Sick and Tired

*When Serving God
Becomes a Burden*

*PAUL
SCHWANKE*

First published by Paul Schwanke, an Independent Baptist
evangelist from Lakeside Baptist Church of Peoria, Arizona.
Evangelist Schwanke is committed to preaching
and providing materials to assist pastors and churches
in the fulfillment of the Great Commission.

Evangelist Paul Schwanke
www.preachthebible.com

Cover design by Mr. Rick Lopez
www.outreachstudio.com

Special thanks to Pastor Ken Brooks

ISBN-13: 978-1505587425
ISBN-10: 1505587425

Printed in the United States of America

CONTENTS

PREFACE *v*

CHAPTER ONE - *God Is Weary With You* *1*

CHAPTER TWO - *Covering the Altar With Tears* *7*

CHAPTER THREE - *Jesus Loves Me But I Don't Care* *11*

CHAPTER FOUR - *It Pays to Serve Jesus* *21*

CHAPTER FIVE - *Return and Remember* *33*

CHAPTER SIX - *On Guard!* *39*

CHAPTER SEVEN - *Prove Me!* *45*

CHAPTER EIGHT - *Today Sir! Today!* *55*

CHAPTER NINE - *They Spoke Often* *67*

CHAPTER TEN - *Last Words* *77*

CHAPTER ELEVEN - *The Silence of God* *87*

ENDNOTES *95*

EVANGELIST JIM MERCER was a mighty preacher of God whose ministry lasted nearly six decades. He had a great passion for the Word of God, often encouraging young students to "know your English Bible." It is a conservative estimate that he spoke directly to several million people, and God used him to lead thousands to Jesus Christ.[1]

With decades of ministry experience behind him, he preached these words:

"Do you know what I am going to do when I go to Heaven? I am going to sit on a rocking chair for a thousand years. And do you know what I am going to do after a thousand years? Then, I am going to start rocking!"

Years ago, I read a book called "Finishing Strong," in which the author challenged men to faithfully serve Christ right up to the finish line. I have over the years observed both in my own life and in others how incredibly difficult it is to 'finish strong.' There are many sins and pitfalls along the way that ensnare and entrap the people of God, and to make matters worse, our own hearts are inclined to deceive us.

I saw some walk a path of immorality. I saw a few get discouraged and quit. But there is something else I noticed. The vast majority never committed an egregious act of wickedness that cost them a ministry or a reputation. They are still in church, still teaching a class, still giving to the Lord's work, and still doing a service for Christ.

But they are worn out. The prospect of joining Jim Mercer on a rocking chair in front of a heavenly Cracker Barrel and rocking for a thousand years is sounding better by the day. We know that we are not to be "weary in well doing" (Galatians 6:9), but we are anyway. That tiredness leads to a sense that we are simply spinning our wheels in the mud which leads to a feeling of frustration in the service of the local church. We are still doing the right thing but it is taking a lot more effort.

Pie Traynor played for the Pittsburgh Pirates in the 1920's and 30's. He was such an exceptional ballplayer that he was the first third baseman to be voted into the Hall of Fame. Although his statistics told the story of a man that excelled both at the bat and in the field, his reputation as a gentleman was even more impressive. In a day when ballplayers were known for their rough living, Pie Traynor was an exception.

As he was known as a man that would never curse, it was a great shock one summer day in 1927 when umpire Pete McLaughlin tossed Pie out of a game against the Brooklyn Dodgers. When the reporters asked the ump why he ejected Traynor, he replied that he was removed from the game because he was not feeling well. When one of the scribes responded that he did not look ill, McLaughlin said, "Pie told me he was sick and tired of my stupid calls."[2]

Sick and tired. A lot of church members understand the feeling.

Some 430 years before Christ was born, the nation of Israel faced the same struggle. Decades earlier their grandfathers and great grandfathers witnessed the horrific razing of Jerusalem by the forces of the Babylonian emperor, Nebuchadnezzar. With the city going up in smoke and the sights and smells of destruction abounding, it seemed as though the nearly 80,000 captives were saying goodbye to Jerusalem for the final time. The funeral dirge they sang is now called Lamentations.

But God was not finished with them. Fifty years later, an amazing Bible prophecy came to pass when Governor Zerubbabel was sent by the Persian King Cyrus back to Jerusalem. Over the years, first the priest Ezra and the n the cupbearer Nehemiah followed his steps to Jerusalem in order to rebuild the temple, the city, and the people.

It would seem that the people would be thrilled at the mighty working of God, but a stubborn complacency became the norm. The prophets Haggai and Zechariah boldly challenged the spiritual lethargy to no avail. The gangrene of indifference had settled in, and a century later it had gotten worse. For all that God had done for them and given them, they were in no mood to return the worship due His name. In His great mercy, God would give them one last opportunity, and should they eschew it, the silence from Heaven would be deafening. It would be centuries before God would speak to them again.

They were getting their last chance. His name was Malachi.

Chapter One

God Is Weary With You

MALACHI WAS the typical Old Testament prophet in that we know very little about him. To the liberal scholars, he didn't even exist. The name means "my messenger" and some modern seminary professors declare that no parent would ever name their child 'Malachi.' God contradicts the experts in the first verse of Malachi: "The burden of the word of the LORD to Israel by Malachi." As usual, either God is right or the professors are right, but they both cannot be right.

It is amazing to read the opening verse of so many of the prophets in the Bible. We have very few if any details about the biographies of Joel, Obadiah, Micah, Nahum, Habakkuk, Zephaniah, Haggai, and Zechariah. For these men, it is all about the message and nothing about the man. "He must increase, but I *must* decrease" (John 3:30).

When the Corinthian church was full of envy, strife, and division, Paul attacked their man-worship with these words: "Who then is Paul, and who *is* Apollos, but ministers by whom ye believed, even as the Lord gave to every man? I have planted, Apollos watered; but God gave the increase. So then neither is he that planteth any thing, neither he that watereth" (1 Corinthians 3:5-7). He went on to tell them while God's ministers are simply plowboys and water-boys, Jesus is everything. All that matters is that "he might have the preeminence" (Colossians 1:18).

Malachi fits in well with the preachers of the Bible who refused to put their name above His name. How offended he would be to discover the ubiquitous 'ministries' today that exalt humans and their titles. There are no 'Malachi Ministries' in the Bible. Messenger-boys don't get the glory.

For the nearly 50,000 Jews who resided in Judah, the political climate was as desperate as the religious climate. A war between the Persians and Egyptians had taken its toll on Jerusalem. The city was destroyed, the conditions were bad, the tax burden was great, and many Jews had to sell their property and even give their children to slavery. Nehemiah was valiantly doing his best to stir the people, but it is easy to see his frustration:

"In those days saw I in Judah some treading wine presses on the sabbath, and bringing in sheaves, and lading asses; as also wine, grapes, and figs, and all manner of burdens, which they brought into Jerusalem on the sabbath day: and I testified against them in the day wherein they sold victuals...I contended with the nobles of Judah, and said unto them, What evil thing is this that ye do, and profane the sabbath day?" (Nehemiah 13:15-17)

"In those days also saw I Jews that had married wives of Ashdod, of Ammon, and of Moab: And their children spake half in the speech of Ashdod, and could not speak in the Jews' language, but according to the language of each people. And I contended with them, and cursed them, and smote certain of them, and plucked off their hair, and made them swear by God, saying, Ye shall not give your daughters unto their sons, nor take their daughters unto your sons, or for yourselves" (Nehemiah 13:23-25).

"Remember them, O my God, because they have defiled the priesthood, and the covenant of the priesthood, and of the Levites." (Nehemiah 13:29).

The political climate, the religious scene, and the home life combined to create a nation in a dangerous state of complacency. It was a mess that few realized and even fewer wanted to fix. By now they were pretty good at turning a deaf ear to the preaching of God's man, whether it be Haggai, Zechariah, or Nehemiah. To compound the problem, they were in the process of accepting human religious traditions in place of the word of God.

"In Malachi's day the people had almost the entire OT, but that was not enough. They wanted an oral law so the rabbis and Pharisees were giving them the Talmud. The Jews were forsaking the Torah (written law of God) for the Talmud (oral law of humans). It would be their undoing."[3]

So Malachi unloads: "The burden of the word of the LORD to Israel by Malachi" (Malachi 1:1). The ministers of our day want to deliver a light and happy message but that was not the command of God to Malachi. As a beast would carry a burden on its back, the message to the people would be a similar heavy load. Worse, the message carried a threat to its listeners. It was like a "dark cloud, heavy with its pent-up fury...prophecies...surcharged with the wrath of God...ready to pour their dreadful contents on those against whom they are directed."[4]

No one could escape the message of God. The first verse of the book indicates that the messages were directed at the entire nation. The message had come from the "LORD to Israel" with Malachi simply being the man in the middle who was nothing but a mouthpiece.

Every segment of their society was exposed to the eye of God. There were messages from God both to the priests (Malachi 1:6) and to the common man (Malachi 2:10). The malaise had stricken them all. Their self-centered thinking caused them to believe the world revolved around themselves, and if God would not make them happy, healthy, and wealthy, then they had no time for Him. Their flippant attitude was exhibited by no less than thirteen challenges they made against God. There was no fear of God nor respect for God. When it came to pleasing God in their worship, in their family, or in their nation, they responded: "Behold, what a weariness *is it!*" (Malachi 1:13)

They had just about had it. The priests were no longer interested in doing their work. The fathers no longer cared about honoring God in their homes. The people were fed up with the whole thing. They were sick and tired.

When we get sick and tired there is something we never stop to consider. Like the people Malachi preached to, we are so self-absorbed with our problems and needs that we never stop to see the bigger, more important picture.

Because our attention and focus is on ourselves, we never stop to consider what God might be thinking.

It must have come as a real shock to the people when Malachi exposed their weary attitude to God and then added these words:

"Ye have wearied the LORD with your words" (Malachi 2:17). That was something they never stopped to think about. They were weary with God but they never imagined that God was weary with them!

No matter where one reads in the Bible, there is always a story or illustration or verse magnifying the patience of God. There are no less than ten verses in the Bible that tell us that God is "longsuffering." The Old Testament word describes anger that is stretched out. A magnificent illustration of the word is found in Ezekiel 17:3: "A great eagle with great wings, longwinged, full of feathers, which had divers colours, came unto Lebanon." The word "longwinged," which pictures a majestic eagle filling the sky with its breathtaking wingspan, is the same word for God's patience and slowness to anger. Though it would be right and just for God to pronounce judgment, He patiently gives multitudes of invitations to return to His blessed mercy and love.

In the New Testament, it is defined as an ability to "remain tranquil while awaiting an outcome."[5]

Our human thinking cannot begin to grasp any attribute of God. To understand His patience with His people in Malachi's day and more so with His people in our day stretches our ability to comprehend.

When Robert Ingersoll, the famous atheist, was lecturing, he once took out his watch and declared, "I will give God five minutes to strike me dead for the things I have said." The minutes ticked off as he held the watch and waited. In about four-and-a-half minutes, some women began fainting, but nothing happened. When the five minutes were up, Ingersoll put the watch into his pocket. When that incident reached the ears of a certain preacher, Joseph Parker, he asked, "And did the gentleman think he could exhaust the patience of the Eternal God in five minutes?"[6]

But even the patience of God comes to an end! Like their forefathers in the wilderness they were provoking God with their attitude, and now God and the people were on an alarming collision course.

They were weary with God and God was weary with them.

Chapter Two
Covering The Altar With Tears

IT WOULD BE A SIMPLE THING to dismiss the people of Malachi's day as backsliders who had forsaken God and gone into the world, but that would be an error. There are many indications in the book of Malachi of people performing outwardly religious acts. If we could somehow move back through time and witness the people of Jerusalem, we might be stunned by the notion that they had tired of God and God had tired of them. It is easy to forget that *"the LORD seeth* not as man seeth; for man looketh on the outward appearance, but the LORD looketh on the heart" (1 Samuel 16:7).

The very first words out of the mouth of the LORD were these: "I have loved you" (Malachi 1:2). Though one might expect that those first words would condemn the people for their ingratitude, they are instead reminded of His marvelous love. "I have loved you" tells the people that God loved them in the past, He loved them in the present day, and He would forever love them. His compassion for them sounded like this:

"For thou art an holy people unto the LORD thy God: the LORD thy God hath chosen thee to be a special people unto himself, above all people that are upon the face of the earth. The LORD did not set his love upon you, nor choose you, because ye were more in number than any people; for ye were the fewest of all people: But because the LORD loved you, and because he would keep the oath which he had sworn unto your fathers, hath the LORD brought you out with a mighty hand, and redeemed you out of the house of bondmen, from the hand of Pharaoh king of Egypt." (Deuteronomy 7:6-8).

On the surface, it would have appeared that the priests of Malachi's day were responding to that love. They were still coming to the altars and offering sacrifices unto God (Malachi 1:7) and they were still blessing the people (Malachi 2:2). It may have been a drudgery to them, but after all, even a priest needs a paycheck. Though their hearts were not in the right place their bodies certainly were.

The people were doing a lot of righteous deeds as well. They were bringing offerings (Malachi 2:12), seeking for the coming Messiah (Malachi 3:1), giving some of the tithes (Malachi 3:10), serving God, keeping His ordinances, and walking mournfully before God (Malachi 3:14). Lest we think they were obstinate and openly rebellious against God, consider the words of Malachi 2:13:

"And this have ye done again, covering the altar of the LORD with tears, with weeping, and with crying out."

The picture is not hard to imagine for a member of a Bible preaching Baptist church. We can almost see the people streaming down the aisle, prostrating at the altar, and weeping before God. We would call such a response a good day at the house of God, yet the Lord saw through the show. He knew they were going to leave the altar and head straight back to their lukewarm lifestyle. He saw through their emotional exhibition discerning the difference between "godly sorrow" and the "sorrow of the world" (2 Corinthians 7:10). God was not fooled.

These words should horrify us because it is so easy to convince ourselves that we are right with God by the chores we perform. "I sing in the choir. I teach a class. I am giving my tithes and offerings. I am serving the Lord. I am OK." Like the people of Malachi's day, our religious actions become integrated into our daily lives and our service to the Lord is no different than mowing the lawn. We do it because it is our obligation to do it. Serving Christ out of a sense of duty is a perilous motivation for the child of God.

Our hearts are so ready to deceive! Before long, actions become a substitute for attitude. Deeds replace a desire to please God. Enough people compliment us on our performance so we allow their platitudes to mix with our self-righteousness, and we convince ourselves that all is right when it is not right. We become mechanical in our work for God and soon we do everything correctly on the outside, but we have lost our heart for God. We find ourselves serving God because we have to; not because we want to. If we need to visit the altar once in a while and cover it with our tears, we tell ourselves that our hearts are still tender before God.

All the while we are sick and tired in the service of the King. And God is sick and tired of our spectacle.

Years ago, the world famous art dealer Sir Joseph Duveen took his daughter to the beach in Dieppe, France. When the little girl dipped her toe into the water, she decided it was too cold and refused to go in. Duveen gathered some sticks, built a small fire on the beach, then placed a borrowed teakettle on the fire. When the water in the kettle was steaming, he poured it in the ocean. His daughter went into the sea without a whimper.[7]

Perhaps we are pouring our kettle of service into the ocean of God's mercy and then convincing ourselves that the water is warm. We play the part we are assigned. As long as the results are there, what does it matter anyway? Soon we are walking on a spiritual treadmill resulting in joyless service and powerless outcomes. We wake up one day to discover how weary the Christian life has become.

We are *sick and tired.*

Chapter Three

Jesus Loves Me But I Don't Care

"I HAVE LOVED YOU." Some 1000 years had passed since the day God freed Israel from the bondage of Egypt. Their liberty was the result of the God who "loved thy fathers" (Deuteronomy 4:37), and the millennium since that mighty miracle demonstrated beyond any doubt His unassailable love. Though they frequently broke His heart and went "a whoring after other gods, and bowed themselves unto them" (Judges 2:17), they could never exhaust His mercy. Like a rainbow shining through the stormy clouds, the love of God preached volumes: "Yea, I have loved thee with an everlasting love: therefore with lovingkindness have I drawn thee" (Jeremiah 31:3).

For all that God had done for them, it would seem impossible that they could ever oppose His love, yet that is precisely what Malachi exposes. One would think God's people would fall on their collective faces in gratitude and praise and honor Him without end, but Israel had another agenda. In Malachi 1:2, they respond: "Yet ye say, Wherein hast thou loved us?" (Malachi 1:3)

What an attitude!

In the 1840's a conman by the name of Alec Hoag lived in New York City. He and his wife invented numerous schemes to steal money from sleeping people and be gone before they knew what happened. Because he never woke the victim and was so quick to escape, he earned the nickname "smart alec."[8]

The etymology books tell us he was the original 'smart aleck,' yet Mr. Hoag had nothing on the people of Malachi's day. They made it their business to habitually question God until they were so backslidden they were actually mocking the love of God.

"Yet ye say" described people primed to engage God in an argument. Like a heckler on the street, they arrogantly challenged the words of God. "Wherein hast thou loved us" are the words of entitled, selfish people that are never satisfied. There are eight occasions in the Old Testament where God showered 'multitudes of mercies' upon His people but that was not enough. Self-centered, egocentric people are never satisfied. They were getting in the face of God and demanding that He show them the evidence of His love for them.

They were not impressed when God revealed how special His love to them really was: "*Was* not Esau Jacob's brother? saith the LORD: yet I loved Jacob, and I hated Esau" (Malachi 1:2-3).

In our lifetimes we have heard innumerable messages and songs about the love of God, but when was the last time we heard about the hate of God? The few ministers who dare preach from these verses try to tap dance around these words as it is quite unsettling to imagine God saying that He hated someone.[9]

But that is exactly what He said.

A great problem is our human issue with the word 'hate.' When we hate, we respond with murder, gossip, anger and other reactions that are sinful in themselves. It is very hard for us to hate and not sin, yet that is not true with God. When He hates, He responds with appropriate judgment, appropriate chastisement, and appropriate condemnation. He can hate and not sin. That is incredibly hard to do as a human.

Esau, the brother of Jacob, has a sordid testimony in the Bible. The words of Hebrews 12:16-17 sum him up well: "Lest there *be* any fornicator, or profane person, as Esau, who for one morsel of meat sold his birthright. For ye know how that afterward, when he would have inherited the blessing, he was rejected: for he found no place of repentance, though he sought it carefully with tears." His life demonstrated a 'profane' attitude toward the will of God and the treasures of God and ultimately it cost him. God promised "his heritage (would be laid) waste for the dragons of the wilderness" (Malachi 1:3). When the Bible describes a land overrun by the wild dragons (jackals, wolves, wild dogs), it is the picture of a desolate wasteland that is uninhabited by humans.

When Esau's descendants, the Edomintes, set out to rebuild, God promised, "I will throw down; and they shall call them, The border of wickedness, and, The people against whom the LORD hath indignation for ever" (Malachi 1:4).

There are a number of verses in the Bible that vividly describe sins that God hates.[10] When a man like Esau or a nation like Edom decided to engage in those sins, they were deciding that they wanted God to hate them. The Edomites were renown in the Bible as a people of pride, treachery, greed, and violence. They rejected God and God rejected them.

When the people wonder how God had loved them, we can hear Malachi preach: "How can you say such a thing? Look what happened to your own brothers when they rejected God. You have committed the same sins yet God has given you opportunity after opportunity. The fact that you have not been consumed by the judgment of God is evidence of His great love. If you doubt it - ask Edom! They are the epitome of a people upon whom the Lord has 'indignation for ever.' The Lord is magnified not because He gave Edom what they deserved, but because He did not give you what you deserve!"

It is easy for us to criticize the Israelites, yet do we not live in a 'what have you done for me lately' society? The difference between the local church of today and those citizens of Jerusalem would be John 3:16. We have before us the history of God's love at Calvary and the day "he sent his only begotten Son into the world, that we might live through him" (1 John 4:9). While there was no excuse for their attitude, our selfishness in the light of the Cross is far more inexcusable. God gave His son to rescue us from Hell, but that is not enough for so many. Their hands are stretched to heaven and they constantly remind God what they need and what He can do for them. Rare is the man that bows his head and says, "Lord, what wilt thou have me to do?" (Acts 9:6)

Sadly, Malachi 1:2 would become the template for the people's attitude throughout the book. This is only the first of eleven such occasions where the people directly confront Almighty God. The others sound like this:

"And ye say, Wherein have we despised thy name?" (Malachi 1:6)
"And ye say, Wherein have we polluted thee?" (Malachi 1:7)
"Yet ye say, Wherefore?" (Malachi 2:14)
"Yet ye say, Wherein have we wearied him?" (Malachi 2:17)
"When ye say...where is the God of judgment? (Malachi 2:17)
"But ye said, Wherein shall we return?" (Malachi 3:7)
"But ye say, Wherein have we robbed thee?" (Malachi 3:8)
"Yet ye say, What have we spoken so much against thee?" (Malachi 3:13)
"What profit is it that we have kept his ordinance?" (Malachi 3:14)
"What profit is it that...we have walked mournfully before the LORD of hosts?" (Malachi 3:14)

In Malachi 1:6 God decries the sins of the priests that had not honored His great name. "A son honoureth *his* father, and a servant his master: if then I *be* a father, where *is* mine honour? and if I *be* a master, where *is* my fear? saith the LORD of hosts unto you, O priests, that despise my name."

A son honoring his father is a son respecting and acknowledging his dad's importance and authority. It was expected that a priest of the Lord would give great credence and weight to the name of God so it would be exalted among the people. Instead of honoring that name they brought shame and disrespect on a steady basis and their disdain for God was evidenced by a careless attitude to the work they had been ordained to do. Their attitude said that serving God was not worth the time nor the trouble.

It is important to note the emphasis on the name of God. Often in the Bible God's name is a synonym for His character and His power. All that God is and all that He does is summed up in His mighty name, but the priests of Malachi's day seemed unaffected. "For from the rising of the sun even unto the going down of the same my name *shall be* great among the Gentiles; and in every place incense *shall be* offered unto my name, and a pure offering: for my name *shall be* great among the heathen, saith the LORD of hosts" (Malachi 1:11).

God wants His name to be "great" everywhere the sun rises and falls, an Old Testament way of saying 'from east to west.' His people in the Old Testament and His people today have been entrusted with the great task of exalting His name so it is known and respected among the unsaved. It was the expectation that the priests who led the nation in worship would understand their duty to keep the service pure and unstained. When pagan nations looked at Israel worshipping God they should have been impressed that God is absolutely pure and holy.

God also wanted His name to be feared. "I *am* a great King, saith the LORD of hosts, and my name *is* dreadful among the heathen" (Malachi 1:14). Even the lost, unsaved people of Malachi's day were to look at Israel and know that their God was to be reckoned with, but the attitude of Israel dimmed their view of God. The priests regularly offered polluted, defiled bread on the altar of sacrifice and dismissed it with the claim that "the table of the LORD *is* contemptible" (Malachi 1:7); "the table of the LORD *is* polluted; and the fruit thereof, *even* his meat, *is* contemptible" (Malachi 1:12). Their job description said they had to offer sacrifices but no paycheck can make a man's heart right. They despised the work; it was so "contemptible" that they "snuffed" at it (Malachi 1:14).[11]

It was too great a chore to bring the appropriate sacrifices that honored God, so their 'worship' digressed until any old bread or any defiled animal would do. What did it matter if the lamb was "blind...lame...(or) sick?" (Malachi 1:8) Such animals may have been injured when they were captured, mauled by another animal, or even have been stolen.[12] They were an Old Testament version of roadkill. We can almost hear a priest say, "Anyone who insists that only proper bread or acceptable lambs can be brought to the temple is too legalistic! It does not matter to God!"

But it did matter to God. In numerous Scriptures He made it clear that a sacrifice had to be without defects and blemishes.[13] He expected them to worship God in the right manner, and when they refused to do so, He called their worship "evil." He told them if they tried to pay their taxes with such animals, the governors would be insulted and reject them out of hand.

We have forgotten that we are required to worship God "in truth" (John 4:24). We give Him a little tip of our time and money and expect that He will be delighted with our efforts. Ministers have conditioned people to think that God is thankful for anything that He can get from us, yet worship that does not bring due honor to Him is still rejected. It is stunning to think that a church full of people can assemble, sing, speak, and give money only to have God pronounce it as 'evil.'

Malachi proceeds to go to the heart of the matter: "And now, I pray you, beseech God that he will be gracious unto us: this hath been by your means: will he regard your persons? saith the LORD of hosts" (Malachi 1:9). They made the mistake of assuming that God would respect them because of who they were, but God is not impressed by someone's title, position, or wealth. "Look at who I am! Look at what I have given! Look at what I have done!" God did not care.

He responded: "Who *is there* even among you that would shut the doors *for nought*? neither do ye kindle *fire* on mine altar for nought." (Malachi 1:10). He did not want their offerings or their gifts or their praises, but rather, He wanted them to shut it down! All of their efforts would come "for nought" as God refused to accept their self-styled worship, and the day was coming when He would ultimately shut the temple doors for good.

I once drove past a church building in Mississippi which advertised their Sunday morning sermon series on a marquee. The pastor was teaching a series of lessons entitled, *"Are You Satisfied With God?"* How "evil!" We have reached depths Malachi never dreamed of as multitudes enter a worship center on Sunday morning bringing polluted and broken sacrifices to God. Religious narcissism is the order of the day with arrogant worshippers demanding that God meet all their needs and desires. They give Him the leftovers and walk away patting themselves on the back for their 'worship.'

The situation was perilous. The priests were defiling the purity of God by treating His work as unholy and profane. The people were following their example by bringing cheap, broken sacrifices, and God was rejecting their watered down religion: "I have no pleasure in you, saith the LORD of hosts, neither will I accept an offering at your hand." It would seem that the condition could not get any worse, yet there is something else they said that compounded the disaster:

"Behold, what a weariness *is it!*" (Malachi 1:13)

They were *sick and tired* and didn't care.

Chapter Four

It Pays to Serve Jesus?

A LITTLE BOY was kneeling in prayer. Obviously disgruntled, he prayed, "Aunt Harriet hasn't gotten married, Uncle Hubert hasn't any work, and Daddy's hair is still falling out. I'm getting tired of praying for this family without getting any results."[14]

Welcome to the ministry. For years I have been privileged to preach around the world with some wonderful saints of God who exemplify the word 'faithful.' I have watched men and women tirelessly serve the Lord simply because they love Him. Sometimes I shake my head in amazement at those who 'keep on keeping on' in a ministry that is unknown and unheralded. No one applauds them, no one honors them, and no one even knows they are there, yet they soldier on.

Then one day it gets to them. It is not a tumultuous event nor a terrifying sin, but they just get tired of serving God. "I keep praying; I keep preaching; I keep working. I am getting tired of not seeing any results."

Malachi dealt with a priesthood and a populace that was just worn out. They had stopped trying to pretend. So they decided to look up to Heaven and inform God they weren't happy with the results. Notice what they had tired of:

They were tired of their Bibles.

God had a covenant with the Levite priests of the Old Testament (Malachi 2:4). As part of that pact, these men were expected to minister to the people, bless the righteous, curse the wicked, carry the ark, and do the priestly functions of the sacrifices. It was a glorious, privileged work, described by Malachi as a covenant "of life and peace" (Malachi 2:5).

For much of the Old Testament the priests were appropriately "afraid before my name," and their attitude was noted by God. As students of the Law, they were constantly ready to dispense God's message, a message that was not in their notes but rather in their mouths (Malachi 2:6). God expected them to "keep knowledge, and…seek the law at his mouth: for he *is* the messenger of the LORD of hosts" (Malachi 2:7). Men who 'keep knowledge" are those who have invested their lives in guarding, protecting, and caring for the Bible.[15]

Their life's testimony backed up their message. "Iniquity was not found in his lips: he walked with me in peace and equity, and did turn many away from iniquity." This is a special commendation. They preached purity and practiced it, and over a lifetime many of the Old Testament priests walked with God as the prophet Enoch had taught them. There was a special heritage these godly men had left behind, and the priests in Malachi's day had a "great cloud of witnesses" (Hebrews 12:1).

But something happened that forced Malachi to preach these disheartening words: "Ye are departed out of the way; ye have caused many to stumble at the law; ye have corrupted the covenant of Levi, saith the LORD of hosts" (Malachi 2:8).

The ministers made a willful, conscious choice to walk a different road. The "old paths" (Jeremiah 6:16) no longer appealed to them, and the result of the compromise was a people who now faced many obstacles. Because they no longer knew the requirements the God of the Bible had for them, the Law was "corrupted." In the minds of the people the Word of God had been annulled and no longer mattered. Soon the ministers became "partial in the law" (Malachi 2:9), delivering a message that was culturally relevant and inoffensive.

It is a dangerous day when God's men get tired of the Word of God. There is a reason the Bible commands a preacher to study like a "workman" (2 Timothy 2:15). A preacher's life work should be an immersion in the Bible. He needs to study it, know it, memorize it, preach it, and practice it.

Preachers get tired of the Bible. Instead of studying for themselves, they buy an book of outlines, find sermons on websites, and toss a message together on Saturday night. Their preaching becomes a tired mixture of the same stories, the same hobby horses, and the same points because they are too bored or too busy to study God's word.

Before long they join the messengers of Jerusalem in delivering selective sermons. They will preach a series such as "How to Have Joy From Philippians." They cherry pick popular verses that will tickle the ears of the listeners all the while ignoring verses that are not so easy to consider. A man who preaches the whole counsel of God will preach the book of Philippians in its entirety. He will preach "rejoice in the Lord," but he will also preach "I am crucified with Christ." He will preach "my God shall supply all your need," but he will also preach "let your moderation be known unto all men." He will preach "I can do all things through Christ," but he will also preach "beware of dogs." He will step into God's pulpit terrorized by the idea of "being partial in the law." A man of God cannot afford to get sick and tired of the book.

They were tired of their marriages.

Most states require two witnesses to sign a marriage license, making it valid. When most people marry, they fail to recognize there is another unseen witness watching the event: "Because the LORD hath been witness between thee and the wife of thy youth…yet *is* she thy companion, and the wife of thy covenant" (Malachi 2:14). God takes wedding vows seriously going so far as to call it a "covenant." In Old Testament days, God was always present as a witness to legal transactions.[16]

When our pagan world laughs at the institution of marriage they are ridiculing a man and woman promising themselves to each other until death parts them. Wicked prenuptial agreements anticipate spouses cheating on their mates. Blasphemous Hollywood media preach adultery and fornication as normalcy. In a world absorbed with self gratification, lying and deceit are accepted practices in our decayed society.

God has a different opinion. When Israel violated their family covenants He chose some vivid language to describe their wickedness. They were dealing "treacherously;" they were "profaning;" they had committed an "abomination" (Malachi 2:10-11). These words paint the picture of a God ready to deal with the wicked.

The Old Testament word "treacherous" refers to someone who does not honor an agreement and acts unfaithfully in relationships. It is used of a husband or wife cheating on their spouse, of a business person breaching a contract, and of the nation of Israel forsaking God and following false idols and religion.[17] Worse, it gives the sense of someone who is covering or cloaking things over; someone who is acting perfidiously in breaking faith.[18] A treacherous person is a liar on steroids. They are living a lie and covering their tracks.

Malachi pointed out they all had "one father." The miracle of Abraham testified to the families of Israel that God had created them, but they shrugged off the standards of God, saying "every man" was cheating. The covenants between Abraham, Moses, and God no longer mattered to the people of the final book of the Old Testament. Treacherous people don't keep their own promises, let alone the agreements of their fathers.

Twice Malachi preached they had "profaned" the Holiness of the Lord. Their dishonesty and lies meant they had made the law of God common and degraded. Their lives were dragging the pure words of God through the mud and filth of the world. God had set them apart for Himself, but they now looked at marriage just like the heathen who bowed before idols. So God called it an "abomination." He absolutely detested their actions.

What were they doing that so offended God? Some were marrying unsaved pagans, a sin Malachi called marrying "the daughter of a strange god" (Malachi 2:11). These were lost women from idolatrous nations who still followed their gods after they were married. According to Ezra and Nehemiah, some of the priests were in such marriages. The Bible does not say how many people had done so, but the number was so great that the whole nation was collectively guilty: "Judah hath profaned the holiness of the LORD" (Malachi 2:12).

Others were divorcing their wives. Malachi called it "putting away" the "wife of thy youth" (Malachi 2:15-16), and God said that He "hateth" it. The men of Jerusalem were so calloused they were tossing away their women like litter on the street. Twice the point is made that they were wives "of thy youth," indicating that these women were not as young as they once were. The old joke of the man who traded his 40 year old wife in for two 20's is not so funny to God.

When a man marries a woman she has become his "companion" and the "wife of thy covenant." God expects her to be a best friend and confidant. A married man has entered into a binding legal agreement with his wife which cannot be frivolously tossed aside, and if he is tempted to do so, he should be reminded that God hates divorce.

In addition to the disobedient marriages and the divorces, violence was an issue. Malachi preached, "For *one* covereth violence with his garment, saith the LORD of hosts" (Malachi 2:16). God expects a man to care for and protect his wife, as so beautifully illustrated in the story of Boaz covering Ruth with his garment. Instead, the men of Malachi's day were covering up their angry acts against their wives with hypocritical spirituality. They convinced themselves they were excused from the standards of God because they were 'masters and scholars.' They thought their generous offerings would act as an indulgence, and if that weren't enough, they would go to the altar and cover it with tears (Malachi 2:12-13).

God had a simple message for them. If they acted violently against their wives, they would have to deal with "the LORD of hosts" (Malachi 2:16). We should take special notice of this particular name of God which is found some 250 times in the Old Testament. "Hosts" refers to armies, so the name depicts Almighty God strapping on the military gear and preparing to fight. His wrath has been aroused and His patience has come to an end. The God of the armies is ready to fight.

If a man engages in a violent act against his wife, he will find that God will fight against him. If a man divorces his wife, he will find that God will fight against him. If a man is unfaithful to his wife, he will find that God will fight against him. God is a great defender of those who are abused and taken advantage of. He is a lover of justice.

It is a warning sign when a Christian is sick and tired of his marriage. If corrective steps are not taken, God will not passively sit by. We will do something about it or He will.

They were tired of seeing the wicked prosper.

Henry Wadsworth Longfellow is quoted as saying, *"Though the mills of God grind slowly, yet they grind exceeding small; Though with patience He stands waiting, with exactness grinds He all."*[19]

We are often frustrated at the timing of God. Our world seems to be out of control as wickedness gains new heights on a daily basis. We tell ourselves it can't get any worse, then the evening news begins. More often than not, it does get worse.

I have had many an unsaved person tell me that God cannot exist because there is so much suffering in the world. A child is abused, a woman is attacked, an act of terror strikes at the heart of a nation, and people convince themselves that if God truly loved people He would never allow such actions.

It is more than a little dishonest when a sinner blames God for the trouble but refuses to acknowledge Him for the blessings. It could also be noted that if we humans simply obeyed the Ten Commandments the evening news casts would become quite boring. A fair person might point out as well that it is more than a little disingenuous to blame God for the results of our society after we have tossed Him out of our schools, our courts, our government, and our living rooms.

Malachi witnessed a similar scenario. When God did not judge the wicked on the timetable of the masses, they said, "Every one that doeth evil *is* good in the sight of the LORD, and he delighteth in them" (Malachi 2:17). Like the blasphemous man today accusing God of not loving people, the citizens of Jerusalem pronounced that God thought that evil was now good and He was enjoying the sin. They had come to this conclusion based on their life experience and like so many humans today, "If I think it - it must be true."

They didn't contemplate how wicked that statement was. Throughout the Bible, God is on record as finding wickedness an abomination, and a human alleging that God is taking pleasure in sin has gone to an evil extreme. Such an indictment accuses God of contradicting His word (Deuteronomy 4:25), a charge that is serious business in the courts of Heaven.

When they cried out, "Where *is* the God of judgment," they were wondering out loud if God was ever going to do something about the wicked and their deeds. No wonder Malachi preached, "Ye have wearied the LORD with your words." When someone wonders aloud when God is going to judge, they better be careful what they are asking for.

In Malachi 3:1, God answers them in the first person. "Behold, I will send my messenger." The vain charges of the people will not stand as the God of the battle responds. His eyes "*are* in every place, beholding the evil and the good" (Proverbs 15:3). "Neither is there any creature that is not manifest in his sight: but all things *are* naked and opened unto the eyes of him with whom we have to do" (Hebrews 4:13). No sin nor sinner has ever found a place to hide from His holy view, and we should never doubt that He will deal with wickedness.

They were tired of serving the Lord.

The people of Jerusalem would not soften. Instead of repenting and seeking forgiveness for their attitude, they doubled down to the place where God said, "Your words have been stout against me" (Malachi 3:13). Earlier their words wearied God but now they had come dangerously close to antagonizing God. 'Stout' words are abusive, arrogant, and aggressive words. Worse, they had spoken out "against" God.

Once again the people of God brazenly responded to the charge of God with a question: "What have we spoken *so much* against thee?" And once again, God responded to them. A casual reader of Malachi might assume that God was out of patience and was finished with the people, but it is enlightening that God constantly responds to the their questions. They may have been arrogant and audacious in their attitude, and the answers they received may not have been what they wanted to hear, but the book of Malachi is a testament to the forbearance of God that desires to see the most haughty backslider return to Him.

He repeated their own words: "Ye have said, It *is* vain to serve God: and what profit *is it* that we have kept his ordinance, and that we have walked mournfully before the LORD of hosts?" (Malachi 3:14) They concluded that all their service for God was empty and meaningless. They spent their lives going to the temple, bringing sacrifices, and giving to God, and now they wondered why. Some had even invested their lives in the service of God and now they were looking at empty bank accounts and they wondered if it was worth it.

When I was a young boy, I remember a little sign my pastor hung in his house. It said, "This is a non-profit organization. It wasn't meant to be, but it sure turned out that way!"

At a revival meeting in Hamburg, Pennsylvania, someone once wrote these words:

It pays to serve Jesus, it pays ev'ry day,
It pays ev'ry step of the way;
Though the pathway to glory may sometimes be drear,
You'll be happy each step of the way.[20]

That song doesn't always line up with real life.

Serving the Lord can be a thankless occupation. A man turns down a scholarship to attend Bible school on his own dime. He sets out to start a church with the change in his pocket. Instead of investing his life in making money, he invests his life in people. When he finally saves some money, there arises a need in the church, and he quietly sacrifices and gives. He gives his energy, his money, his time, his health to the work of God, and one day he looks in the mirror and sees the graying hair, then looks at his bank account and sees a tiny, inadequate number, and he would not be human if he didn't wonder what could have been. In a moment of weakness he says, "Was it all in vain?"

Every servant of the Lord comes to such a moment of honesty. Usually, the question is not boldly verbalized like

Malachi's people did, but it is in the heart nonetheless. While we may not be prone to sing Mr. Hutson's song, the heart of faith in a moment of doubt does have another song deep inside. It was written in 1941 by a woman suffering great affliction:

Oft times the day seems long, our trials hard to bear,
We're tempted to complain, to murmur and despair;
But Christ will soon appear to catch His Bride away,
All tears forever over in God's eternal day.

Sometimes the sky looks dark with not a ray of light,
We're tossed and driven on, no human help in sight;
But there is one in heav'n who knows our deepest care,
Let Jesus solve your problem - just go to Him in pray'r.

Life's day will soon be o'er, all storms forever past,
We'll cross the great divide, to glory, safe at last;
We'll share the joys of heav'n - a harp, a home, a crown,
The tempter will be banished, we'll lay our burden down.

It will be worth it all when we see Jesus,
Life's trials will seem so small when we see Christ;
One glimpse of His dear face all sorrow will erase,
So bravely run the race till we see Christ.[21]

It is the only way to make sure we don't get *sick and tired*.

Chapter Five

Return and Remember

A FOOLISH OLD FARMER, so the story goes, concluded that the oats he had fed his mule for years were simply costing him too much. So he hatched a plan: he mixed a little sawdust in with the feed, and then a little more the next day, and even more the next, each time reducing the amount of oats in the mix. The mule didn't seem to notice the gradual change, so the farmer thought things were fine and kept decreasing the proportion of oats. But weeks later, on the day he finally fed the poor beast nothing but sawdust, the mule finished the meal and fell over dead.[22]

So goes the curse of 'gradualism.' Men like Ezra, Nehemiah, and Malachi knew the stories of old and the accounts of the mighty working of God. They often reminisced of a time when God was moving mightily in their nation and His name was revered and known. Slowly but surely, they, like us, were moving away from God.

It was time for solutions. One reason I believe in giving an invitation at the conclusion of a preaching service stems from the belief that the God of the Bible left room for a decision to be made. It is not preaching until the man of God says, "What will ye do?" (Hosea 9:5) There are too many illustrations in books like Jonah and Amos where God stands ready to show boundless mercy. Until the moment that a sinner is lost in Hell there is hope that "all should come to repentance" (2 Peter 3:9). Until the very moment the wrath of God finally falls there is a possibility: "Who can tell *if* God will turn and repent, and turn away from his fierce anger, that we perish not?" (Jonah 3:9)

God knew the people were sick and tired, so after diagnosing the problem, He is ready with the prescription. The answers for Jerusalem four centuries before Jesus came are the same answers for the local church twenty four hundred years later.

God told them to return and remember.

Throughout the Bible, the first step for a backslidden child of God is to take inventory of his condition, remember where he has fallen from, and return to that place. Evangelist Vance Havner once preached from Revelation 2:5: "Remember therefore from whence thou art fallen, and repent, and do the first works." He said, "A revival is the church remembering, the church repenting, and the church repeating." It is a frequent point made in the Bible in both the Old and New Testament, and Malachi was no exception.

"Return unto me, and I will return unto you, saith the LORD of hosts" (Malachi 3:7). "Remember ye the law of Moses my servant, which I commanded unto him in Horeb for all Israel, *with* the statutes and judgments" (Malachi 4:4).

Return to the Lord. Remember the Bible. We tend to seek new answers but God said, "I *am* the LORD, I change not" (Malachi 3:6). Malachi preached that God's love for Israel never wavered and it was the single reason "ye sons of Jacob are not consumed." He then told them the "ordinances" (Malachi 3:7) of God had not changed. His love never changes and His word never changes! In our unstable age what a comfort that is.

Samuel Arbesman, a complex systems scientist, recently wrote a book entitled *The Half Life of Facts.* In the world of science facts have an "expiration date." Truth will only be truth until there is a new truth discovered and it is only a matter of time before a new science book will be needed.

"The half-life in physics is about 10 years. Other researchers have even broken this down by subfield, finding a half-life of 5.1 years in nuclear physics, 6 years for basic solid state physics, 5.4 years in plasma physics, and so forth. In medicine, a urology journal has a half-life of 7.1 years, while plastic and reconstructive surgery is a bit more long-lived, with a half life of 9.3 years."[23]

To which God responds: "Being born again, not of corruptible seed, but of incorruptible, by the word of God, which liveth and abideth for ever" (1 Peter 1:23).

Sadly, as He consistently invites us to return, we often answer like the people of Jerusalem: "But ye said, Wherein shall we return?" The self-righteousness of the people blinded them from their backslidden condition. Like many today who frequently sit in an auditorium and listen to the preaching of the Bible, the people heard but never responded to Malachi. We can almost hear them say, "What have I done to offend God? Where did I ever leave Him? Why should I humble myself before Him?" They wondered aloud why they needed to return since in their minds they had never gone away.

It is interesting that God told Malachi's listeners to remember "the law of Moses my servant." There is no other occasion in the Old Testament where Israel is exhorted to remember God's law.[24] Though there are some forty times that Moses is called the servant of the Lord, this verse and Daniel 9:11 are the only places where this phrase is found in the prophets.

When the preacher mentioned Mount Horeb, which is also known as Mount Sinai, the importance of the verse would not be lost upon them. Horeb was not only the place where Moses received the commands from God; it was also home to the cave where the illustrious prophet Elijah met with God. From many different angles God wanted their attention.

He reminded them that the Scriptures were the "statutes and judgments", two words often used in the legal profession. Their fathers had entered into a serious contractual agreement with God and they were not about to be excused simply because they were worn out. "If a man vow a vow unto the LORD…he shall not break his word, he shall do according to all that proceedeth out of his mouth" (Numbers 30:2). "Better *is it* that thou shouldest not vow, than that thou shouldest vow and not pay" (Ecclesiastes 5:5). God expects His people to keep their word.

If we surrendered to do the Will of God and follow Him, He has the right to expect us to keep our promise. It is not acceptable for us to put our hand to the plow and begin working for Jesus only to turn back because we are sick and tired. Being weary in the service of Christ does not give a license to forsake vows and lie to God.

Return to the Lord. Remember the Bible.

A missionary in Africa, Charles Greenaway, was having a terrific struggle. His work load was heavy and his wife was seemingly sick every day. Few or none were being saved, so the discouraged missionary asked God to send him home. He considered himself a failure. Then he pictured Calvary. The wounded hands and flowing blood seemed to say, "I preached the same message and they rejected me. So why don't you follow me and leave the results in my hands." That was the day Charles Greenaway won a critical victory that kept him serving Christ for decades.

When he told the story, a pastor named Ira Stanphil wrote:

I traveled down a lonely road and no one seemed to care,
The burden on my weary back had bowed me to despair,
I oft complained to Jesus how folks were treating me,
And then I heard him say so tenderly,

My feet were also weary upon the Calvary Road,
The cross became so heavy, I fell beneath the load.
Be faithful weary pilgrim, the morning I can see,
Just lift your cross and follow close to me.

I work so hard for Jesus I often boast and say,
I've sacrificed a lot of things to walk the narrow way,
I gave up fame and fortune, I'm worth a lot to thee,
And then I heard him gently say to me,

I left the throne of glory, and counted it but loss,
My hands were nailed in anger, upon the cruel cross
But now we'll make the journey with your hand safe in mine,
So lift your cross and follow close to me.[25]

Weary pilgrim, *return to the Lord and remember the Bible.*
It is where a Christian begins to get the victory when he is
sick and tired.

Chapter Six

On Guard!

WHEN I WAS PREACHING in Papua New Guinea, the missionary explained that pagan men were expected to 'try the garden' before they married. In our sophisticated society such a phrase would be politically incorrect, so we use the word 'compatible.' It is pretty much the same thing with one major difference.

'Compatible' in our pagan civilization means to find out if the 'partner' is going to please me, satisfy me, care for me, and meet my needs. One of the most often listed reason for divorce is that my spouse "is no longer attractive to me."[26] Of course, this is nothing new as Malachi condemned that same attitude 2440 years ago.

In the jungles, however, the men have a different view of 'compatibility.' They want to take their potential wife on a test run and see if she is able to produce children, particularly males. If she can, they will marry. If she can't, he will toss her aside.

It might be argued, that as repulsive as their brand of adultery is, it probably makes more sense than America's blatant fornication.

When the men of Jerusalem were weary of their marriages and tossing their wives aside, the man of God preached a powerful point. "And did not he make one? Yet had he the residue of the spirit. And wherefore one? That he might seek a godly seed. Therefore take heed to your spirit, and let none deal treacherously against the wife of his youth" (Malachi 2:15).

We might hear Malachi preach: "Don't you understand what happened when God took you and your wife and made you one? He expects the marriage to last! He expects the family to leave a residue of righteousness long after you are gone. He expects a seed of children that will follow the Lord and live a godly life. Marriage is a lot bigger than your feelings and your pride! You cannot shrug your shoulders and throw it all away just because you are tired of the whole thing!"

He goes on to tell a husband what to do when he is tired of the home. "Therefore take heed to your spirit, and let none deal treacherously against the wife of his youth." Malachi is preaching that a man needs to be on guard and pay special attention to his spirit. This is a concept that very few men consider yet it is critical for a husband who is *sick and tired*.

When we hear of marriages that crumble and couples heading to divorce court, it is usually assumed that some moral sin is responsible. A lot of preaching to men correctly warns of the dangers of dirty web sites and internet temptations. Our society has become obsessed with filth and it is nearly impossible to avoid it.

But God warns a man to protect his spirit.

Evangelist Ron Comfort has often preached, "Adultery has slain its thousands, but bitterness has slain its tens of thousands." He is so accurate. A man may assume all is well because he has never cheated on his wife, has an internet filter, and has never gone to a house of sin, but Satan has plenty of other weapons in his arsenal. It would be impossible to calculate the marriages that have been ruined by a bitter spirit.

Every Christian husband should take special notice of Colossians 3:19: "Husbands, love *your* wives, and be not bitter against them." Had most of us written the Bible, we would not have penned those words. We would write, "Husbands, love your wives, and do not cheat on them." But God recognizes the havoc bitterness creates in a Christian home and the angry husband who holds it all in. He never erupts in a rage of violence, he never chases an immoral fling, but he lives with a sour disposition and cancerous attitude. So God commands: "Love your wife." Then he states: "Be not bitter." For good measure He adds: "Take heed to your spirit."

The book of Proverbs identifies other 'spirits' and destructive attitudes a husband can harbor. He must be careful to avoid a "hasty" or an impatient spirit (Proverbs 14:29). If he does not watch his words he will develop a "breach in the spirit", a spirit that is broken and fractured (Proverbs 15:4). If he allows his heart to be full of sorrow and pain he will have a "broken" or crushed spirit

(Proverbs 15:13). We will never know how many homes have been destroyed by a "haughty" spirit (Proverbs 16:18). No one can bear to live with a man who has a "wounded spirit" (Proverbs 18:14). If he does not "rule over his own spirit" he will be like a city without walls (Proverbs 25:28).

What a list! A marriage can be damaged by a husband who insists that it must be his way and it must be right now. Cruel and angry words that can't be taken back can do irreparable harm. A feeling of self pity, a haughty arrogance, or a spirit out of control can make as big a mess as any sordid affair can.

For a Christian husband trying to do right the question would be asked, "How can I have the right spirit?" Thankfully, the Bible does not only tell us what to do but also gives us instruction on how to do it. There are many texts where a man could turn and gain Holy Spirit insight on guarding his spirit, and it would be wise to search and study them. Colossians chapter 3 is one such example. Notice the commands a man who wants to forsake bitterness discovers when he studies his Bible:

"Set your affection on things above" (Colossians 3:2).
"Mortify therefore your members which are upon the earth" (Colossians 3:5).
"But now ye also put off all these" (Colossians 3:8).
"Put on therefore" (Colossians 3:12).
"Let the peace of God rule in your hearts" (Colossians 3:15).
"Let the word of Christ dwell in you richly" (Colossians 3:16).

"Whatsoever ye do in word or deed, do all in the name of the Lord Jesus" (Colossians 3:17).

What a powerful blueprint God has given us to keep the bitterness out of our life! He says there are sins our flesh desires that need to be obliterated. Others need to be put off like a man takes off his jacket. There are virtues that need to be put on, a Bible that needs to live inside, and a Savior who needs to be our first priority. It is never easy to "rule" our spirit yet there is help in God's Word. We have to patiently learn and put into practice what God has given us.

We know the great frustration of trying to live a pure life. Romans 7 remains in the Bible as the guarantee that our flesh and our spirit are constantly at odds, but there are choices laid out in the Bible for a Christian man to study and practice. We can live in victory and we can allow God to change us. He is more than willing to turn a sour marriage sweet.

While it is necessary for a husband to set standards of moral purity, it is equally important for him to set barriers around his spirit. If he doesn't, it won't be long before he gets *sick and tired* of his marriage.

Chapter Seven
Prove Me!

IN THE 1970's, a Dallas pastor wrote these words in his weekly column:

The population of this country is 200 million. Eighty-four million are over 65 years of age, which leaves 116 million to do the work. People under 20 years of age total 75 million, which leaves 41 million to do the work. There are 22 million who are employed by the government, which leaves 19 million to do the work. Four million are in the Armed Forces, which leaves 15 million to do the work. Deduct 14,800,000, the number of state and city office employees, leaving 200,000 to do the work. There are 188,000 in the hospitals and insane asylums, so that leaves 12,000 to do the work. Now it may interest you to know there are 11,998 people in jail, so that leaves just 2 people to carry the load. That's you and me - and, brother, I'm getting tired of doing everything myself.[27]

The population numbers have grown some 50% but the workload still seems the same. We are trying to do more with less and for all of the technological advancements, hard workers have less time than ever. Before long we find ourselves in a rut doing the same things over and over. It is the same job, the same activities, the same thing at church, the same problems, and the result is a Christian who is bored and dulled.

So it is time for a challenge. It is almost like being taken back in time to recess at the schoolyard. The words and insults are flying back and forth until it is time for somebody to prove his manhood. "I dare you" would be followed by a "double dog dare." On occasions there might even be a "triple dog dare" which only a coward could refuse. The challenge is given and it was time to 'take up the gauntlet.'

God is issuing a challenge to us humans with the words "Prove me" (Malachi 3:10). He is inviting us to turn the tables on Him.

Frequently the Bible reminds us that God is putting us to the test and examining our lives. David cried out, "Search me, O God, and know my heart: try me, and know my thoughts: And see if *there be any* wicked way in me, and lead me in the way everlasting" (Psalm 139:23-24). We have the perpetual need of God exposing the sin in our lives and displaying the way to go. Yet, in Malachi 3, God is actually inviting us to examine Him. He wants us to put Him to the test and see if He is as good as His word. This is such an extraordinary verse that we cannot afford to ignore the offer. Imagine it! God is daring us to prove Him!

Sick and tired people start getting cheap with God. When the people of Jerusalem did so, God simply told them "ye have robbed me" (Malachi 3:8). Naturally, they questioned His question: "Wherein have we robbed thee?" Came the answer from Heaven: "In tithes and offerings."

When they were keeping back the money that rightfully belonged to God they were robbers. Tithing was not some 'legalistic' command found in Leviticus, but rather a practice of righteous people as far back as Abraham.[28] The word 'tithe' means the tenth part, and righteous Israelites were very careful to give to the Lord what belonged to Him. If there were ten lambs one was given to God. If there were ten pieces of fruit one was laid aside.

Offerings were used to care for the priests, to construct the tabernacle and the temple, and to care for the needs of the work of God. While the tithe was mandatory for Israel, the size of the offerings was up to the discretion of the giver. Malachi 3:8 made it clear that God expected both. They were expected to recognize that the blessings of God were not an entitlement, and that they should express their gratitude with gifts beyond what was required.

The result of their stinginess meant that they were "cursed with a curse" (Malachi 3:9). When the Old Testament uses such a repetition of words it is a way of saying that there was a great curse upon them, a curse that extended to "this whole nation." Such judgments in the Bible stemmed from human sinfulness and it was always God who was the executor of the penalty.[29]

Israel was infected with lethargy. It was a chore to put their tithe in the offering plate so God issued His challenge. That challenge still works for the worn out Christian today. It is so easy to be trapped by the 'same ole same ole'. We go to Sunday School every Sunday morning at the same time. We listen to the same teacher with a different lesson that pretty much sounds the same. We go to the auditorium where we sit in the same seat every week. We stand for the opening hymn and prayer, sit while the choir sings, stand again for the next hymn, sit and ignore the announcements, put a tithe envelope in the offering plate, stand one more time to sing, sit while someone sings a special, and then listen to the message. It is the same thing on Sunday night and the same thing on Wednesday night. We might have a responsibility in the nursery, the classroom, or the bus route, and we do our duty, only to start the same procedure the next week.

So God says, "Prove me!" He shakes us up by going right to the heart. "For where your treasure is, there will your heart be also" (Luke 12:34). We can almost hear Him say, "If you are tired of the mundane let's see if you are willing to see what I can do in your life. If you want some excitement let's see if you are willing to trust me with your most valued riches. Let's see what can happen when you put me to the test!"

If we listen closely, we can almost hear Him say, "I dare you!"

Are you willing to take Him up on His offer? You trusted Him with your soul, will you trust Him with your wallet? Now that He has issued the challenge will you step up and accept it? Perhaps one reason we are *sick and tired* stems from our fear to shake up our life. Maybe we secretly like being *sick and tired* because it is a path of no resistance.

So God issues the challenge:

Be a tither. It is a great place to start. Don't be a tipper, be a tither. Instead of determining what we think we can afford, hold your nose, jump in the deep waters, and start with ten percent. God said to bring "all the tithes" (Malachi 3:10). It is not "all the tithes that are left after we pay our taxes." It is not "all the tithes that are left after I pay my bills." The challenge of God is to be a ten percent tither.

"You don't understand. I can't make ends meet now!" God said, "Prove me." "But I have medical bills." God said, "Prove me." "But I have a mortgage to pay." God said, "Prove me."

Be a bringer. God did not tell the people to send a check in the mail, He told them to "Bring ye all the tithes." Too many backslidden Christians soothe their conscience by giving their money but not themselves. When we begin to enjoy the fun of giving we will want to be a part of the program. "Bring ye" is the command of God.

Tithe at the storehouse. The "storehouse" was the place of supplies. It was probably a special warehouse in the temple complex where goods were stored until they were distributed.[30] God said the storehouse was located in "mine house." The command then was to bring the tithe that belonged to God to the house of God.

So what is the house of God? In the Old Testament the phrase is found eighty-five times. Every one of those occasions describe the physical place where Israel would go to worship God.[31] With one exception (Jacob in Genesis 28:17), it referred either to the temporary tabernacle or the permanent temple where God's people attended.

The phrase "house of God" is found six times in the New Testament. The first three occurrences, found in the Gospels, quote Old Testament Scriptures referring to the Tabernacle. The other three verses tell us that the "house of God" is now the New Testament Local Church:

"But if I tarry long, that thou mayest know how thou oughtest to behave thyself in the house of God, which is the church of the living God, the pillar and ground of the truth" (1 Timothy 3:15).

"And having an high priest over the house of God" (Hebrews 10:21).

"For the time is come that judgment must begin at the house of God: and if it first begin at us, what shall the end be of them that obey not the gospel of God?" (1 Peter 4:17)

When David tithed he brought the money to the Tabernacle. When Nehemiah tithed he brought the money to the Temple. When we tithe we bring the money to the local church. Don't send your tithe to a minister on TV. Don't send your tithe to a school. Don't send your tithe to an organization that is outside of the local church. In fact, don't send your tithe anywhere. Bring it to the house of God - the local church.

Make His needs more important than our needs. Malachi told the people to tithe so that "there may be meat in mine house." Their giving provided sustenance for the priests serving God. When they tithed they were putting God's business ahead of their own business. Tithing is a great way for a Christian to "seek...first the kingdom of God, and his righteousness" (Matthew 6:33).

One of the greatest givers in human history was a humble, unnamed widow who lived in a Phoenician coastal village called Zarephath. The days were desperate as an excruciating famine was dominating the land. The story finds the woman gathering a pile of sticks to make one last meal. All hope is gone as she says, "I *am* gathering two sticks, that I may go in and dress it for me and my son, that we may eat it, and die" (1 Kings 17:12).

The man of God Elijah challenges the woman to prove God. "Fetch me, I pray thee, a little water in a vessel, that I may drink...bring me, I pray thee, a morsel of bread in thine hand." It would not have taken much for the woman to politely turn down the request. She could have reasoned her responsibility to her son outweighed the needs of the preacher but she does not. Like the people of Malachi's day she had a promise from God: "For thus saith the LORD God of Israel, The barrel of meal shall not waste, neither shall the cruse of oil fail, until the day *that* the LORD sendeth rain upon the earth" (1 Kings 17:14). She acted on that promise.

"And she went and did according to the saying of Elijah: and she, and he, and her house, did eat *many* days. *And* the barrel of meal wasted not, neither did the cruse of oil fail, according to the word of the LORD, which he spake by Elijah" (1 Kings 17:15-16).

The woman took the dare! God's man and God's work was more important than eating, and the result was not only a woman who ate during famine, she remains an example to us 2900 years later.

Malachi tells us what to expect from God should we choose to prove Him. We get to go first. Are we willing to make His work more important than ours? Are we willing to give back to Him what He has given us? If so, God makes a promise: "(See) if I will not open you the windows of heaven, and pour you out a blessing, that *there shall* not *be room* enough *to receive it*. And I will rebuke the devourer for your sakes, and he shall not destroy the fruits of your ground; neither shall your vine cast her fruit before the time in the field, saith the LORD of hosts. And all nations shall call you blessed: for ye shall be a delightsome land, saith the LORD of hosts" (Malachi 3:10-12).

The first time God opened the 'windows of heaven' was in the days of Genesis 7:11. The next statement says, "And the rain was upon the earth forty days and forty nights." If we wonder if God is able to meet our needs if we give, all we need to do is ask Noah if it rained enough. As there was no room to receive the water, a tither who trusts God with his finances will find there is not enough room to store the blessings of God!

But God is not done. He told people living in an agricultural society, "And I will rebuke the devourer for your sakes, and he shall not destroy the fruits of your ground" (Malachi 3:11). God is saying, "If you take care of my business then I will take care of your business."

There is more. "And all nations shall call you blessed: for ye shall be a delightsome land" (Malachi 3:12). For Israel that meant God would so bless them that the nations of the world would look at them and admire how good they had it. God promised to care for them and prosper them to the place where He would point at them and tell the world, "That's what happens to a nation that I delight in!"

That will fix the "sick and tired" problem! Show me someone weary with God, and it probably has been a while since God delighted in them. If you look at the checkbook it will most likely indicate a man that hasn't proven God in a while. So when you are ready to break out of the lethargy, do it with your money. After all, "Where your treasure is, there will your heart be also!"

Years ago, a young man surrendered his life to be an African missionary, but as the time of departure drew near, he discovered his wife could not stand the climate. He was heartbroken, but he prayerfully returned to his home and determined to make all the money he could to be used in spreading the Gospel around the world. His father, a dentist, had started a side business where he made a drink for his church's communion service. The young man took the business over and developed it until it assumed vast proportions. His name was "Charles Welch," and Welch's

Grape Juice was marketed around the world. He gave hundreds of thousands of dollars to the work of missions.[32]

So if you are *sick and tired*, why not take the challenge? What do you have to lose except your weariness?

Chapter Eight

Today Sir! Today!

CENTURIES AGO AN ENTIRE CHURCH found itself in grave danger. It is not that they were preaching a false Gospel or tolerating corrupted doctrine, for Jesus commended their convictions. They were hard workers, they stood against false teachers, they faithfully taught the Bible, and they patiently bore a lot of trouble for Jesus. From the outside they appeared to be the model church without any error or deficiencies, but there was one item that threatened them so Jesus exposed it.

"Thou hast left thy first love" (Revelation 2:4).

It is the signature problem for *sick and tired* Christians. As the church of Ephesus demonstrated, outward actions can mask inward conditions. We can lead exemplary lives, stand for right, fight the battle against wrong, and labor for Jesus while having abandoned the love we once had for Christ.

In 1918, a missionary gave a pamphlet about loving Christ to Helen Lemmel. As she read the words her heart burned within her and these words poured from her soul:

Turn your eyes upon Jesus,
Look full in His wonderful face.
And the things of earth will grow strangely dim
In the light of His glory and grace.[33]

Malachi's answer for the sick and tired of his day was the same as Pastor John's message to the Church of Ephesus. When your heart has turned cold and distant, get back to your first love for your Savior. Should we desire to "turn our eyes on Him," the book of Malachi gives us a wonderful portrait to consider.

Israel had become *sick and tired* of waiting for God to judge the wicked (Malachi 2:17). They had turned aside to the point where they were challenging God with the words, "Where *is* the God of judgment?" The mighty God of the armies responds to their anger with these words: "Behold, I will send my messenger, and he shall prepare the way before me: and the Lord, whom ye seek, shall suddenly come to his temple, even the messenger of the covenant, whom ye delight in: behold, he shall come" (Malachi 3:1).

In Malachi's day, it was common for a visiting king to send a messenger ahead to announce his coming. That messenger would prepare the way literally and figuratively. If there were physical obstructions in the way of the coming king they would be removed. If there were logistical issues to be worked out, he would take care of it.

When the citizens of Jerusalem wondered where the God of judgment was, Malachi prophesied that John the Baptist would come. He would go to the wilderness, preach a mighty message, and challenge people to turn from their sin to the Savior. As a messenger-boy, John had one message. He would make the way plain. He would remove the obstacles. He would point men to the Savior. Should there be any question, John summed up his place with seven words: "He must increase, but I *must* decrease" (John 3:30).

Then Malachi preached a favorite message of God's men down through the corridor of time. It was the theme of the Old Testament prophets, the promise of New Testament apostles, and it remains a passionate point of God's preachers today.

"Jesus is coming!"

The people of Malachi's day were looking to the coming of Christ in much the same way we are looking for His coming today. When He came the first time, He was laid in the manger in Bethlehem. When He comes the next time, it will be in the clouds to call out His saints. When He comes the third time, He will return to the Mount of Olives and rightfully take His place as the King of Kings. His coming is in three stages, yet to people of the first century, the people of our day, and the people living through the Tribulation there are common themes that apply.

He is coming suddenly. Malachi preached on one of the most neglected points of the coming Christ: "the Lord...

shall suddenly come" (Malachi 3:1). We often hear preachers say, "Jesus is coming soon," yet that phrase is not found in the Bible. When Malachi preached of the coming Lord there was an urgency in his tone that told the people they should be looking with anticipation, yet Jesus did not come for more than four centuries. The Apostle Paul was "looking for that blessed hope" (Titus 2:13); Peter was "looking for...the coming of the day" (2 Peter 3:12); and John could only say, "Even so, come, Lord Jesus" (Revelation 22:20); but each of those men met their Savior through the portal of the grave.

When Malachi preached on the suddenness of the Lord's coming, he was telling people in every generation to be looking, waiting, and expecting the Lord to come. When Jesus was born in Bethlehem, there were very few anticipating that event. He caught them all by such surprise that King Herod had to instruct the foreigners to "search diligently for the young child" (Matthew 2:8). When he comes in the clouds, it will be "in the twinkling of an eye" (1 Corinthians 15:52), leaving no time to get ready. When He returns to reign, the whole world will be stunned to "see the Son of man coming in the clouds of heaven with power and great glory" (Matthew 24:30).

The very last words that human ears on this earth have heard from the lips of Jesus are these: "Surely I come quickly." He did not say, "I am coming soon." When he comes there will be no time to prepare. The lost man will have no time to fall on his knees and call on the name of Christ. The backslidden Christian will have no time to clean up his life. The saint with 'good intentions' will have no time to fulfill the many promises he has made to God. No wonder the Bible says that if someone is anticipating the quick return of Christ, he will "(purify) himself, even as he is pure" (1 John 3:3).

Two thousand years have come and gone, yet the righteous man is still looking for Him. He does not look to a spectacular, date-setting preacher who gives the latest 'signs of the times'. He does not dial in an internet radio station to get the latest updates. All he knows is that Jesus said to expect Him today. All he needs is the Bible to prepare his heart.

The story is told of the traveler who was visiting European cities. His passion was castles, and at one Scottish castle he found incredibly beautiful gardens and immaculately kept grounds. When he saw the gardener working the flower bed, he approached him and commended him for the fine work. Without stopping, the gardener thanked him for the compliment. When the visitor remarked, "The owner of the castle must be pleased with your efforts," the worker responded, "He has not been here for more than ten years." The amazed tourist remarked, "You must be expecting him soon." Came the reply: "I expect him today sir! Today!"

The doubter may say, "It has been a long time since Jesus left. When do you expect him?" The righteous respond, *"Today sir! Today!"*

He is coming certainly. Malachi left no doubt as to the fact of His coming. Repetition in the Old Testament is one of the greatest methods of emphasis, so we get the passion of the preacher when he said, "the Lord, whom ye seek, shall suddenly come to his temple, even the messenger of the covenant, whom ye delight in: behold, he shall come, saith the LORD of hosts" (Malachi 3:1). What a message! "The Lord…shall…come…behold, he shall come." There is no room for doubt.

He will come as the "messenger of the covenant." Ancient negotiations were often carried out through messengers going back and forth between the parties. The emissary would carry the message for the master.

The coming Jesus brings a message from His father. In the first century, He came "to seek and to save that which was lost" (Luke 19:10). When He comes in the clouds, the saved will might "meet the Lord in the air: and so shall we ever be with the Lord" (1 Thessalonians 4:17). When He comes as king, He will return "in flaming fire taking vengeance on them that know not God, and that obey not the gospel" (2 Thessalonians 1:8).

No wonder the Bible says the righteous "delight" in His coming! The wise men from the east "rejoiced with exceeding great joy" (Matthew 2:10). The Christian will cry, "Death is swallowed up in victory" (1 Corinthians 15:54). The Tribulation saint will shout, "Redemption draweth nigh!" (Luke 21:28) All of the sorrows, pain, and tears will vanish at the sight of Him!

"Today sir! Today!"

He is coming powerfully. The rebel challenged Malachi with the words: "Where *is* the God of judgment?" Now the man of God says, "Let me tell you where He is:"

"But who may abide the day of his coming? and who shall stand when he appeareth? for he is like a refiner's fire, and like fullers' soap: And he shall sit as a refiner and purifier of silver: and he shall purify the sons of Levi, and purge them as gold and silver, that they may offer unto the LORD an offering in righteousness. Then shall the offering of Judah and Jerusalem be pleasant unto the LORD, as in the days of old, and as in former years. And I will come near to you to judgment; and I will be a swift witness against the sorcerers, and against the adulterers, and against false swearers, and against those that oppress the hireling in his wages, the widow, and the fatherless, and that turn aside the stranger from his right, and fear not me, saith the LORD of hosts. For I am the LORD, I change not; therefore ye sons of Jacob are not consumed" (Malachi 3:2-6).

Malachi focused on the second coming of Christ in judgment. On that day, no one will abide His coming. Many proud and obstinate people have blasphemed and mocked the name of Jesus, but in the moment of His return, they will no longer be able to hold on. All of their taunts, all of the times they used His precious name in vain, and all of His loving invitations they rejected will come crashing upon them as they see Jesus in power and glory.

The long battle will end when He comes. The phrase "who shall stand" pictures a military scene with two great armies poised to go to war. On one side of the battle field stands Satan and his invisible forces joining with the armies of the world. On the other side stands the "LORD of hosts". It will be no contest. "These shall make war with the Lamb, and the Lamb shall overcome them: for he is Lord of lords, and King of kings" (Revelation 17:14). At last the wicked will be forever defeated.

"Today sir! Today!"

He is coming to purify. He will clean things up in a hurry. A "refiner's fire" was a smelting furnace that would be used to remove impurities from precious metals. A "fullers' soap" was a powerful chemical agent with a strong cleansing effect. In everyday terms it may be more like modern bleach than modern soap.[34]

Notice that it will be so easy for Him that He is going to "sit *as* a refiner and purifier." The smiths of that time sat bending forward over their small melting furnaces to ascertain from the color of the metal whether it was pure. The Lord will refine his people just as peacefully and expertly as a silversmith.[35] He will have all the time He needs to do the job right. There is no panic with Him. He will keep removing the impurities until He is finally satisfied with the finished product.

The object of his cleansing will be the "sons of Levi." The result will be that "the offering of Judah and Jerusalem (will) be pleasant unto the LORD, as in the days of old." The impurities that have defiled modern worship will be long gone in the smelting pot of the holiness of God's fire. His name will finally be adored and worshipped in honor.

"Today sir! Today!"

He is coming to judge. When reading the Bible we often fly through verses and never consider them, but there is an ominous message in verse five: "And I will come near to you to judgment." The arrogant thought that God was ignoring evil, but now He is coming near. Picture an angry God rising in wrath and humans shrinking the closer He comes. It is a statement of horror.

It turns out that God did see the wickedness and now He is calling them out. He said, "I will be a swift witness" (Malachi 3:5). The trial, the verdict, and the execution of sentence will not take long. No slick lawyer will get a motion for delay of trial. He specifically names four classes of the wicked that He will judge: "the sorcerers...the adulterers...(the) false swearers... (and) those that oppress."

Sorcery was forbidden in the nation of Israel from the early days of Exodus. These were people that would attempt to control the spiritual world with incantations, charms, and spells. They were so offensive to God that He lumped them in a list that included evil parents who sacrificed their children to pagan gods (Deuteronomy 18:9-11).[36]

The men who were dealing treacherously with their wives would discover that God hates adultery. It didn't matter then and it doesn't matter now if 'everybody is doing it.' God said: "Marriage *is* honourable in all, and the bed undefiled: but whoremongers and adulterers God will judge" (Hebrews 13:4).

False swearers would be called perjurers in our day. Their lying was worse because when invoking the name of God in their oath, they were saying, "With God standing by my side as a witness I am saying the truth." Then they would turn around and tell a boldface lie. When a witness lays their hand on the Bible and proceeds to lie, he had better consider these words: "the word that I have spoken, the same shall judge him in the last day" (John 12:48). That very Bible men treat as a prop is going to come back and condemn them.

The oppressors bullied the hirelings, the widows, the orphans, and the strangers in the land. Hirelings were day workers that expected payment at the end of the day. If a boss refused to make that payment, God said He would exact it. Because widows and orphans did not have an advocate to plead for them, corrupt judges often refused to hear their case. God promised to defend them. The foreigners would often be taken advantage of, but there are no less than ten Old Testament Scriptures that warn Israel against abusing them.[37]

Malachi exposed the reason they committed these sins when he said, "(Ye) fear not me." They acted as if they would never meet the Holy God of the Bible. They mistreated those who were lower on the social scales, believing they could get away with it; but at the end of the day, they did so because they did not fear God. Now God rises from His seat to execute justice.

"For I *am* the LORD, I change not" (Malachi 3:6). Governments change but God does not. Religions change but God does not. Social standards change but God does not.

In October of 2014 Pope Francis signaled a change in the Roman Catholic view of homosexuality and divorce wanting to "adapt to 'changing conditions of society.' In defending the acceptance of sin, the pope stated: 'God is not afraid of new things.'"[38]

God has a message for the Pope: "For I *am* the LORD, I change not." We can place our confidence in His word and His stability.

A *sick and tired* Christian has stopped looking for the return of His Savior, but the promises of Malachi are real today. We have this guarantee from the lips of Jesus, "I will come again" (John 14:3). When He comes with a fan in His hand "he will throughly purge his floor, and gather his wheat into the garner...(and) burn up the chaff with unquenchable fire" (Matthew 3:12). He comes looking for the man that "purifieth himself, even as he is pure" (1 John 3:3), and when He returns, the wicked will learn the hard way that "the Father...hath committed all judgment unto the Son" (John 5:22).

The sceptic says, "Those words were spoken a long time ago! Society has changed a lot since then!" The simple response from Scripture says:

"Jesus Christ the same yesterday, and to day, and for ever!" (Hebrews 13:8)

When Jesus comes to reward His servants,
Whether it be noon or night,
Faithful to Him will He find us watching,
With our lamps all trimmed and bright?

Oh, can we say we are ready, brother?
Ready for the soul's bright home?
Say, will He find you and me still watching,
Waiting, waiting when the Lord shall come?[39]

"Today sir! Today!" Such is the cry of the Christian who loves the appearing of Jesus. Such is the cry of the Christian who is listening for the trump. Such is the cry of the Christian who can't afford to be *sick and tired.*

Chapter Nine
They Spoke Often

IT LOOKED like an ordinary apartment building to me. Swirling around it in dizzying speed was the traffic of one of the largest cities in the world. Masses of people with blank stares walked streets that seemed to go in a million different directions. It was tall and colorless, and from the outside it was no different than the rest of the buildings that all seemed to touch the sky.

My Chinese friend and I walked through the glass door and into a tiny elevator. It rumbled up more than thirty stories and stopped with a jolt. I stepped into the hallway and looked at a host of doors leading into a myriad of apartments. Throughout the land of China there must have been countless similar buildings with literally millions of similar apartments. I remember thinking how glad I was to have a guide at my side. It would be impossible to find such a place on my own.

He opened the door and we walked into a small flat. One of the tiny bedrooms was called the nursery, another was the Sunday School class, and the living room was the auditorium. One by one precious folks rode that same elevator until it was time to begin. The singing, the fellowship, and the Christian joy was extraordinary.

It was an astounding experience. Like a grain of sand on the beach, that little assembly was surrounded by more than 23 million people. Most would never know they were there nor would they care. But God is not like 'most.' God knows every burden of every member in that local church and He watches with pleasure as they gather.

There was a similar group in Malachi's day. When reading his book it is tempting to sink into the state of malaise that had gripped the people. It would appear that nobody cared, that everyone was lackadaisical and lukewarm, and that the preacher was wasting his time. Then we come to Malachi 3:16:

"They that feared the LORD spake often one to another."

There were those who still wanted to honor God.

We make a grave mistake when we think God is impressed by our massive church buildings, wealthy endowments, and complex programs. He never required stained glass windows, stately pipe organs, million dollar artwork, or robed choirs. We humans may be wowed by the latest technology but not Him. He despises the 'big business' of modern religion and a concept of 'worship' that comes straight out of Hollywood.

But there is something that He looks for.

"Then they that feared the LORD spake often one to another." Religion is so complex, but God simply looks for people who fear Him. "The LORD taketh pleasure in them that fear him, in those that hope in his mercy" (Psalm 147:11). "Behold, the eye of the LORD *is* upon them that fear him, upon them that hope in his mercy" (Psalm 33:18).

That little group of 'God-fearers' gathered together frequently and spoke to each other. Their words caught His attention and the Bible says "the LORD hearkened, and heard *it.*" What a glorious thing! We remember our Sunday School teachers singing, "Oh be careful little tongues what you say." A Bible preacher who preaches "all the counsel of God" (Acts 20:27) will find himself frequently condemning gossip and griping and guile. We remind the saints *"there is* not a word in my tongue, *but,* lo, O LORD, thou knowest it altogether" (Psalm 139:4). But that is a two way street. It is true that He hears the shameful and evil words, but He also hears the conversation of those who gather and speak of Him.

God was not only impressed enough to hear them, He did something about it. "A book of remembrance was written before him for them that feared the LORD, and that thought upon his name." This is the only time the Bible uses the phrase "book of remembrance." Such a book was common in ancient palaces when a king would hire a secretary to record historical events. The book of Esther describes a king calling for his book to recall deeds done on his behalf. In Malachi, we can picture "the divine King surrounded by his heavenly servants instructing a scribe to record an event in the royal archives."[40]

Of course God never forgets, yet the picture is still marvelous. He does not need reminding, but we need to be reminded that He doesn't need reminding. This precious book describing the tiny remnant that is not ashamed of His name is "before him." It is constantly right in front of Him as a continual reminder of His faithful servants who fear Him. In the book of Malachi, the dominant attitude of human arrogance is on display some thirteen times as the people blatantly challenge God. Now God finds the few that are not accusing Him, but are fearing Him, and He has a promise for them:

"And they shall be mine, saith the LORD of hosts, in that day when I make up my jewels; and I will spare them, as a man spareth his own son that serveth him. Then shall ye return, and discern between the righteous and the wicked, between him that serveth God and him that serveth him not" (Malachi 3:17-18).

We have been conditioned to think that God does not take sides. When election season is upon us, (which seems to be 364 days per year), politicians and journalists take it upon themselves to speak for God and ostentatiously report, "God is not a Republican and God is not a Democrat." Dead religion presents a passive God who stands idly by watching the affairs of men. But that is not the God of the Bible. He does takes sides.

When God saw the small remnant who feared Him, thought of Him, and spoke of Him, He openly took their side: "they shall be mine." He did not say that of the critics who questioned His every move, nor of the robbers who held back what was His, nor of the ministers who despised His name. He did look at the small group that was "not ashamed" (Romans 1:16) and said, "This is my crowd." To those people He made some promises:

God promised He would "make up (His) jewels." As a woman guards her most prized gems, God said these people held a special place in his jewelry box. When the wrath of God would fall upon the earth for the sins of the people, God promised to "spare them." He would show compassion on them and protect them. Often it seems the judgment of God is indiscriminate, judging everyone in its way, but God said that when the great day of His judgment comes it will be easy to "discern between the righteous and the wicked, between him that serveth God and him that serveth him not" (Malachi 3:18).

That will be evident during the time of Tribulation when the "the day cometh, that shall burn as an oven" (Malachi 4:1). The foundations of the earth will be rocking as the furnace of God's wrath opens. Those who are on His wrong side will run from Him: "And the kings of the earth, and the great men, and the rich men, and the chief captains, and the mighty men, and every bondman, and every free man, hid themselves in the dens and in the rocks of the mountains; And said to the mountains and rocks, Fall on us, and hide us from the face of him that sitteth on the throne, and from the wrath of the Lamb" (Revelation 6:15-16). Those who are on the right side will run to Him: "And then shall they see the Son of man coming in a cloud with power and great glory" (Luke 21:27).

Sometimes it is hard for us to tell the difference, but God knows how to distinguish the chaff from the wheat. One day it will be simple for humans as well to discern between the righteous and the wicked, between the servants and the selfish, between the jewels and the "stubble."

God promised He would burn the wicked. Malachi has been very bold in identifying them. He called out the sorcerers, adulterers, perjurers, and the oppressors. Now he preached that "all the proud, yea, and all that do wickedly" will face the furnace of God's wrath. Notice the emphasis on the word "all." Malachi's contemporaries were convinced that elements in society were getting away with their sin, but God guaranteed that "all" of them would face Him. Like the dry, brittle stalks left in the farmer's field, they will be highly flammable. The Day of God's Judgment will be the day of accounting.

We are often angered when a criminal is set free by a dishonest judge. He walks out of the courtroom taunting the law and mocking people that love right. We see powerful politicians set themselves above the laws they write and make themselves the exceptions to their own rules. We are *sick and tired* of watching evil triumph, yet God made a promise. The day is coming that the evil man will no longer flaunt his sin. One day he will be "cast into the lake of fire" (Revelation 20:15). There is coming "the day" when justice wins.

God promised He would send the "Sun of righteousness." What a contrast! The wicked man will see the burning fires of a raging Hell, but the righteous man will see the brilliant sun of God's righteousness coming in glory. "But unto you that fear my name shall the Sun of righteousness arise with healing in his wings" (Malachi 4:2).

Though the Son of God has numerous titles in the Scriptures, there is something special about "Sun of righteousness." The gloominess of sin has created a society where "men (love) darkness rather than light, because their deeds (are) evil" (John 3:19). Convinced the cover of night can hide their depravity, humans persuade themselves that God does not see nor know. "Every one that doeth evil hateth the light, neither cometh to the light, lest his deeds should be reproved" (John 3:20).

But there is coming the ultimate day when Jesus returns to the earth to sit upon His throne. "For as the lightning cometh out of the east, and shineth even unto the west; so shall also the coming of the Son of man be" (Matthew 24:27). To look upon Jesus on that day would be the same as staring at the sun on a cloudless day. The brilliant glory bursting upon the earth will leave petrified humans frozen in their tracks unable to respond to Him. How foolish the armies of the world will look as their massive weapons of destruction melt in His presence. Instantly, arrogant humans will be subdued, and those who taunted Him and profaned Him will comprehend how omnipotent He is. The professor who denied Him, the minister who disdained Him, the human who derided Him - all will fall before the glorious Son of God in abject terror.

It will bring the reversal of the ages. The discouraged and broken will now "go forth, and grow up as calves of the stall." Like a pony set free to gallop in the meadow, the oppressed victim of evil will now run and leap with great joy. The oppressed will "tread down the wicked" so that they are "ashes under the soles of your feet" (Malachi 4:3). Burnt in the fire of God's oven, the wicked tormenters will be nothing but "mounds of ashes beneath the triumphant feet of God's saints."[41]

Once more we are reminded: "in the day that I shall do *this*, saith the LORD of hosts." It would not happen soon enough for the critical scorners in Malachi's day; it will not happen soon enough for the critics in our day. Yet, in God's perfect timing, He will perform as He promised. 'The Day' will be the moment the wicked are repaid and the righteous are recompensed.

"They that feared the LORD spake often one to another." It would seem that the few that still fear Him have a lot to talk about. Malachi joins Zechariah and Paul in reminding us that it is not the mighty nor the powerful nor the wise nor the noble. From the day that Noah stood against the whole world to our present hour, history demonstrates that God is able to work "by many or by few" (1 Samuel 14:6).

In March of 1858, a bold young preacher, Dudley Atkins Tyng, stood before a crowd of 5000 men in Philadelphia. His text for the day was Exodus 10:11: "Go now ye *that are* men, and serve the LORD." God used the message in a mighty way as more than 1000 responded to the Gospel invitation. The entire city was affected and the Spirit of God was moving.

The next week Tyng returned to his family in the country where he witnessed the operation of a corn-thrasher in his barn. When he raised his arm to assist a mule, the loose sleeve of his morning gown was caught between the cogs. Tyng's arm was lacerated severely, the main artery severed, and the median nerve injured. The preacher was rushed to a hospital but efforts to save him were in vain. Six days later he went home to Heaven.

As he lay dying in the hospital, a multitude of broken hearted men came to the hospital to pray for him. Sensing that his son was on the precipice of eternity, his father asked him if there were any last words for the men. Dudley Tyng said, "Stand up for Jesus, father; stand up for Jesus; and tell my brethren of the ministry, wherever you meet them, to stand up for Jesus." With those words he went to meet the Savior for whom he stood.

At his memorial service his pastor concluded the message with the words of a poem he had written to remember the preacher:

Stand up, stand up for Jesus! Ye soldiers of the cross;
Lift high His royal banner, It must not suffer loss;
From vict'ry unto victory, His army shall He lead,
Till ev'ry foe is vanquished, For Christ is Lord indeed.

Stand up, stand up for Jesus! The trumpet call obey;
Forth to the mighty conflict In this His glorious day;
Ye that are men now serve Him against unnumbered foes;
Let courage rise with danger, And strength to strength oppose.

Stand up, stand up for Jesus! The strife will not be long;
This day the noise of battle, The next the victor's song;
To him that overcometh A crown of life shall be;
He with the King of Glory Shall reign eternally.[42]

This is not the time to wallow in self pity. This is not the time to sit idly by. This is not the time to allow ourselves to be *sick and tired*. This is the time to fear Him and speak of Him. This is the time to stand up for Jesus!

Chapter Ten

The Last Word

IT WAS A BATTLE like no other. As the Amalekites were attacking the recently freed Hebrews, Moses commanded General Joshua, "Choose us out men, and go out, fight with Amalek." He continued, "To morrow I will stand on the top of the hill with the rod of God in mine hand" (Exodus 17:9). As long as Moses was able to lift the rod, the Israelites prevailed in the war. When his tired arms sagged, the enemy advanced. At last Aaron and Hur supported the heavy hands of Moses, and "Joshua discomfited Amalek and his people with the edge of the sword" (Exodus 17:13). Victory was theirs.

As momentous as that campaign was, something far more important came from it. It would be easy to miss, but in truth, it was one of the most significant commands human ears have ever heard: "And the LORD said unto Moses, Write this *for* a memorial in a book" (Exodus 17:14).

For forty years God had prepared Moses in the Pharaoh's palace in Egypt. It started with his miraculous rescue at the Nile River where it was evident that the presence of God was upon his life. As a young boy in the king's castle, he no doubt played with the mechanical toys so popular with the Egyptian children. As he grew, he may have fallen in love with the beautiful horses of Egypt, perhaps riding them on hunting excursions. We know little of Moses' young life but there is this insight: "And Moses was learned in all the wisdom of the Egyptians, and was mighty in words and in deeds" (Acts 7:22).

God had a purpose. A wealthy boy living in Egypt fifteen centuries before Christ would spend countless hours sitting in a classroom reading and writing scripts. He not only learned curriculum but also multiple languages, and when he 'graduated' at age 40, he was mighty in his ability to speak and work. Moses was a brilliant man.

When God spared a little baby in the Nile, it was impossible for his parents, Amram and Jochebed, to see what lay ahead. There were many things that God needed from that boy. He required a leader of men; a tireless worker; a man of principles; a bold preacher. But there was another requisite, so God allowed a little boy to be adopted from a Hebrew family into Egyptian royalty where he received a world class education.

God needed a writer.

When the victory against Amalek was procured, God told a prepared Moses to "write...in a book." For the next forty years, Moses would keep on writing the words that proceeded "out of the mouth of God" (Matthew 4:4) until the Pentateuch, the first five books of the Bible, was completed. We can imagine Moses getting alone with God, carefully opening his parchment, dipping his pen into the ink, and writing, " In the beginning God" (Genesis 1:1). And he doesn't stop until he goes home to glory.

We fast forward more than 1000 years and Malachi is listening to the final words of the Old Testament. Between Moses and Malachi were no less than twenty-nine humans that God used to record His words. Some were kings and some were paupers. Some lived in the big city of Jerusalem and some lived in podunk villages. Some were preachers and some were singers. Those humans and their stories remind us yet again that "God hath chosen the foolish things of the world to confound the wise" (1 Corinthians 1:27).

The Old Testament walks us up the rocks of Mount Sinai. We marvel at the faith of an old man willing to forsake family and friends to go to the Mediterranean desert where God makes of him a mighty nation. We revel in the roller coaster account of an honored son who falls into a pit of slavery whose life is spared only to be tossed into jail who then becomes Prime Minister. We hear a trembling little boy say, "Speak; for thy servant heareth." We see the stone fly through the air into the forehead of Goliath. We pick up a songbook containing 150 hymns we still sing today. We still listen to the wise proverbs of a king instructing his son how to avoid the pitfalls of life. We stand on a mighty mountaintop and witness the fire of God fall upon an altar and lick up the water coursing from the crevices of the altar. We witness a backslidden preacher run to the ends of the world to avoid the will of God, only to meet up with a mighty whale. We weep with a heartbroken prophet whose wife abandons him to run after lovers. We feel the heat and hear the crackle of the fire as three boys are tossed to the flames. We wait in breathless anticipation as a king asks a lowly servant, "Is thy God…able to deliver thee from the lions? We watch the conversion of a priest into a prophet who then becomes a watchman for the house of Israel. The adventures never stop, for behind them all is the living God of Heaven and Earth who "hath done great things for us; *Whereof* we are glad" (Psalm 126:3).

Now we come to the final message of the Old Testament. How could these powerful Scriptures possibly come to an end? What is the final message that God would have for His people? The message reads like this: "Lest I come and smite the earth with a curse" (Malachi 4:6).

The last word of the Old Testament is *"curse."* That single word was so frightening and convicting to the Jewish scholars, they placed verse five after verse six so their Scriptures would not end with a curse.[43]

It does not simply say there will be a curse, it says that God will "smite the earth" in judgment. The last message of the Old Testament is God threatening to wipe the earth out.

That is not how we like our stories to end. We want a happy, upbeat ending. We want the good guy to win, the bad guy to lose, and then everybody living happily ever after.

What a difference Jesus makes! When we come to the last statement of the New Testament, Pastor John reminds us, "The grace of our Lord Jesus Christ *be* with you all" (Revelation 22:21). Because of Calvary and the empty tomb, we have the privilege of knowing the grace of God instead of the curse of God. Well did John sum up the message of the entire Bible with the single word: "Amen!"

From the moment sin entered into the world in Genesis 3, the word "curse" indicated the judgment of God. For the sin of Adam and Eve, the ground was cursed, the serpent was cursed, and worst of all, humanity was cursed. The Old Testament uses the word some 174 times reminding us of the holy judgment of God. As Malachi preaches the final message to a people *sick and tired* of serving God, it would seem to be very appropriate. They had tired of God and now they would be cursed.

Surrounded by such a people, Malachi had a final message for the handful of the faithful that still feared the Lord. When they were prone to discouragement or even fear for the events of their day, the preacher told them to lift up their eyes and look for someone: "Behold, I will send you Elijah the prophet" (Malachi 4:5). The final promise of the Old Testament informed the Hebrews that one of their mightiest prophets was returning to the earth.

The phrase "I will send" has a sense of imminency to it. Elijah would come when they were not expecting him, so they should have the attitude of the Scottish gardener. As Malachi concludes the Old Testament Scriptures, God is telling righteous people to be on the lookout for Elijah.

This is a fascinating prophecy that has a duel fulfillment. In Matthew 17 the disciples of Christ point to this verse and ask, "Why then say the scribes that Elias must first come?" The Savior responds: "Elias truly shall first come, and restore all things. But I say unto you, That Elias is come already, and they knew him not, but have done unto him whatsoever they listed." They readily "understood that he spake unto them of John the Baptist" (Matthew 17:10-13).

John the Baptist was the intended fulfillment of Malachi's prophecy, but his coming came with a caveat. "*If ye will receive it, this is Elias, which was for to come*" (Matthew 11:14). He came preaching repentance and the kingdom of God, informing the people that Jesus had come and they had a choice to make. Would they accept Him as their Messiah and king? Sadly, their response is found in John 1:11: " *He came unto his own, and his own received him not.*" The "great and dreadful day of the LORD" (Malachi 4:5), the day when the wicked are judged and King Jesus sits on His millennial throne, would be postponed.

But God is not finished. One day the skies will be filled with the glory of Jesus returning to the earth in judgment and authority. He is coming to reign in power. As God prepares the world for that day, He promises to send two witnesses who will preach for 1260 days. The satanic-infused world government will try to stop them, but fire will proceed "out of their mouth, and (devour) their enemies" (Revelation 11:5).

Bible students often debate the identity of these two witnesses, but the best case can be made that they are Elijah and Moses. Elijah is the easiest to identify because he is prophesied to come in the book of Malachi. It will be a great Biblical reminder when they "shut heaven, that it rain not in the days of their prophecy." As Elijah did before an evil King Ahab so will he do in the days ahead. They will also "have power over waters to turn them to blood, and to smite the earth with all plagues, as often as they will" (Revelation 11:6). We are quickly reminded of the days of Exodus when Moses plagued the land before an arrogant Pharaoh.

What a message for the *sick and tired*. Like preachers of today, we can hear Malachi pleading with the people to return to the faith of their fathers, men like Abraham and Moses and Samuel and David and Elijah. One day God promises to "turn the heart of the fathers to the children, and the heart of the children to their fathers" (Malachi 4:6). The King of kings and Lord of lords will restore this wicked world to the intentions of God as the LORD finally takes His rightful place on the throne.

Not long after the Civil War, a beloved preacher named John Jasper pastored the Sixth Mount Zion Baptist Church in Richmond, Virginia. Someone asked him if there had been five preceding Mount Zion Baptist Churches but he said, "No, we just liked the name." He was preaching one day on the glory of Heaven, and as he attempted to describe the scene, he was so caught up with emotion that he could not talk. As the people sat in the pews with respectful silence he tried several times to speak but nothing happened.

Soon the tears were rolling down his cheeks but the words would not come. He shook his hand towards the doors inviting the people to leave but they sat there enthralled. He tried to leave the auditorium to go to his study but still they sat there.

The preacher finally composed himself, stepped to the edge of the pulpit, and preached these words:

"Brothers and sisters, when I think of the glory which shall be revealed in us, I can visualize that day when old John Jasper's last battle has been fought and the last burden has been borne. I can visualize that day when this tired servant of God shall lay down his burdens and walk up to the battlements of the City of God. Then as I stand outside the beautiful gate, I can almost hear the Mighty Angel on guard say, "John Jasper, you want your shoes?"

"I'se gonna say, "Course I wants ma shoes, ma golden slippers to walk the gold-paved streets of the City of God, but not now."

"Then I can hear the Mighty Angel as he says, "John Jasper, don't you want your robe?"

"I'se gonna say, "Course I wants ma robe, that robe of linen clean and white which am the righteousness of the saints, but not now."

"Then the Angel would say, "John Jasper, you want your crown?"

"I shall say, "Course, Mighty Angel, I wants all the reward that's comin' to me, this poor black servant of the Lamb, but not now."

"Then the Angel would say, "John Jasper, wouldn't you like to see Elijah, the great prophet, who called down fire from heaven? Wouldn't you like to shake hands with John the beloved disciple who leaned on the Master's breast at the Last Supper? Wouldn't you like to meet with Paul, the great apostle to the Gentiles, the greatest church establisher and soul-winner of all time?"

"I'll say, "Course, Mighty Angel. I wants to know and to shake hands and to commune with those, the saints of God who have won the incorruptible crown. Yes, I have some loved ones over here I wants to see, too, but not now. Fust, I wants to see Massa Jesus…I wants to see Him fust of all." [44]

When we are tempted to be throw in the towel we should go to the last chapter of the book. We cannot quit, we cannot be discouraged, and we cannot fail Him. We must press on and abound in our labors for Christ confident that it will be worth it all one day. When we are *sick and tired* we do well to remember the words of Horatio Spafford:

And, Lord, haste the day when my faith shall be sight,
The clouds be rolled back as a scroll;
The trump shall resound, and the Lord shall descend,
Even so, it is well with my soul! [45]

Chapter Eleven

The Silence of God

THE HISTORY OF ISRAEL is an amazing story that is still being written. The Old Testament stands as a tribute to this message of God: "The LORD did not set his love upon you, nor choose you, because ye were more in number than any people; for ye *were* the fewest of all people: But because the LORD loved you, and because he would keep the oath which he had sworn unto your fathers, hath the LORD brought you out with a mighty hand, and redeemed you out of the house of bondmen, from the hand of Pharaoh king of Egypt" (Deuteronomy 7:7-8). It is a history of the amazing love of God and His unchanging Word.

Faithful Malachi joined the legions of men who declared His message to His people. Though each biography is different, the common thread relates the story of human men who put their lives, their fortunes, their futures, and their all on the altar of sacrifice. Their innumerable invitations line the pages of the Old

Testament as God "plead(s) with you…and with your children's children" (Jeremiah 2:9).

It was time for a *sick and tired* people to respond to the call of God. Would they repent? Would they respond? Would they return?

We might say that Malachi 4:7 records their choice. Of course there is no verse 7, and in most Bibles, the next page between the Old Testament and the New Testament is blank. That blank page preaches a mighty message.

They would not come home. They chose complacency. They ignored the invitation. Their *sick and tired* condition would rule their lives.

The blank page stands for 430 years of the silence of God. For more than four centuries God did not speak to them. When we go to the Jewish history books the picture is not pretty.

The mighty prophets of God were replaced by scholars and higher critics. They thought nothing of adding to the words of God with hypocritical rules and restrictions described in Matthew 23:4: "For they bind heavy burdens and grievous to be borne, and lay *them* on men's shoulders; but they *themselves* will not move them with one of their fingers." Their religion of works gradually produced a deep apostasy and the few righteous that were left were fighting a losing battle.

The political climate worsened as well. The wars were many and the bloodshed was great. The notorious Greek king, Antiochus Epiphanes, nicknamed the 'madman', sacrificed a pig on the altar in Jerusalem and built a shrine to the pagan god Zeus. He refused to allow Jewish parents to circumcise their children, the Sabbath was outlawed, and every known copy of the law was burned.[46]

There is a price to pay when we get *sick and tired*. When we spurn His invitations and pleadings there will come a payday which can take many forms. For Israel, it was 430 years of silence. Dead silence.

430 years. 156,950 days. Silence.

And then one day an old, old man joined a company of priests in the temple. In those days there were twenty-four courses (orders) of the priests. Twice a year, for a week at a time, these men would be responsible for the service of the temple. The old man's order was known as the course of Abia, and though these particular priests had a rather notorious reputation, this man was righteous and blameless. In his time it is estimated there may have been some 18,000 priests living in Jerusalem, and to most of them, the work at the temple simply put food on the table and paid the rent. This old man, however, had an impeccable testimony of obeying the commands of God.

The old man watched as the lots were about to be cast. The 'lots' may have been coins, sticks, or dice that would be used to make a random selection. The winner of that lottery would have a special privilege indeed. He would be selected to step into the Holy Place (second only in reverence to the Holy of Holies) and offer incense as part of the sacrificial offering. A priest could only be selected once in his life for this honor and for the old man time was running out. With only two opportunities per year, he must have thought he had a better chance of being hit by lightening.

To his astonishment, the lot fell upon him. How thrilled he must have been. If only his wonderful wife could know! With the exception of the high priest who entered into the Holiest, no other human could ever be this close to God. Most priests would never experience this honor, and it was forever out of the reach of non-priests.[47]

It was about 3:30 in the afternoon when he took the censer in his hand and went into the temple of the Lord. A whole multitude of people would remain outside that Sabbath day praying, "May the merciful God enter the Holy Place and accept with favor the offering of his people." As they prayed, the old man offered the incense.

Then it happened. In an instant, the silence of God came to an end. 430 years of waiting had come to this moment in time, and God finally had a message for His people. The angel of the Lord Gabriel, who was last seen in the Bible conversing with Daniel, suddenly stood on the right side of the altar. A stunned priest listened to the first words from God that human ears had heard in more than four centuries:

"Fear not" (Luke 1:13).

What words! The last word a human heard from God in the Old Testament was the word "curse." The first words a human heard in the New Testament were "fear not." When the theme is the judgment of the Holy God who will not excuse sin, there is a lot to fear. When the message looks to the day when the fiery wrath of God will take "vengeance on them that know not God" (2 Thessalonians 1:8), human knees will buckle and human hearts will tremble. But Heaven was stirring. Soon another angel would say, "For unto you is born this day in the city of David a Saviour, which is Christ the Lord" (Luke 2:11). Fear not!

The old man could not believe his ears. As amazing as the appearance of Gabriel was, the next statement may well have stopped his heart: "Fear not, Zacharias: for thy prayer is heard; and thy wife Elisabeth shall bear thee a son, and thou shalt call his name John." There is no thing too hard for the Lord! There are no people too old for the Lord!

Gabriel went on: "He shall go before him in the spirit and power of Elias, to turn the hearts of the fathers to the children, and the disobedient to the wisdom of the just; to make ready a people prepared for the Lord" (Luke 1:17).

Elijah was coming! God kept His word to His people. His final promise of the Old Testament said, "I will send you Elijah the prophet before the coming of the great and dreadful day of the LORD" (Malachi 4:5). His first promise of the New Testament was "thy wife…shall bear a son."

The New Testament starts where the Old Testament stops. Though human promises fail, we know that the word of our God will abide forever. When we are discouraged and ready to quit, God has given us a book of His promises that will never pass away. The old priest Zacharias summed it up best: "Blessed *be* the Lord God of Israel; for he hath visited and redeemed his people…to perform the mercy *promised* to our fathers, and to remember his holy covenant" (Luke 1:68-72).

He does not forget. He will remember His word.

When the discouragements are mounting and the enemy is gaining, the strong child of God has one book that sustains him. He does not require a new philosophy, a new pedagogue, or a new program. He looks to an old, black book that has proven itself reliable through the centuries of time. He takes his stand on the eternal, unshakeable words of God. He craves a revival of a love for the Bible.

It is God's prescription for the *sick and tired.*

[1] profilerministries.com

[2] Forr, James. *Pie Traynor: A Baseball Biography.* Jefferson, North Carolina: MacFarland & Company Publishers. 2010.

[3] Phillips, John. *Exploring the People of the Old Testament (3).* Grand Rapids, Michigan: Kregal Publications. 2007.

[4] Moore, T. V. (1856). The Prophets of the Restoration, or, Haggai, Zechariah, and Malachi: Commentary (p. 337). New York: Robert Carter & Brothers.

[5] Arndt, W., Danker, F. W., & Bauer, W. (2000). A Greek-English lexicon of the New Testament and other early Christian literature. Chicago: University of Chicago Press.

[6] Jones, G. C. (1986). *1000 illustrations for preaching and teaching* (pp. 146–147). Nashville, TN: Broadman & Holman Publishers.

[7] Behrman, S.N. (1951). *Duveen: The Story of the Most Spectacular Art Dealer of All Time.* The contents of the book originally appeared as a series of articles in *The New Yorker.*

[8] Cohen, G.L. (1985). *Studies in Slang Part 1.*

[9] One scholar criticized Malachi as "lacking depth." Others have tried to soften the message by pointing to a polygamist who loves one wife more than another in Deuteronomy 21 where the terms of 'love' and 'hate' are used in comparison - the hated wife is the one less loved. *(See The New International Commentary on the Old Testament: the Book of Malachi by Pieter Verhoef)*

[10] Deuteronomy 12:31; 16:22; Jeremiah 44:4; Hosea 9:15; Zechariah 8:17; Psalm 5:5; 11:5; Isaiah 61:8; Amos 5:21; Proverbs 6:16-19.

[11] 'Snuff' is a verb indicating to blow, to breathe, to boil. It is used of projecting one's breath but in a figurative sense of God blowing the breath of life into Adam (Gen. 2:7). It refers to a fire that is not blown, meaning not fanned to expand it (Job 20:26). In this context it is a picture of extreme disrespect. *(The Complete Word Study of the Old Testament)*

[12] Verhoef, Pieter R. (1987). *The Books of Haggai and Malachi.* The New International Commentary on the Old Testament, ed. R.K. Harrison and Robert L. Hubbard, Jr. Grand Rapids, Michigan: William B. Eerdmans.

[13] Exodus 12:5; 29:1; Leviticus 1:3; 22:20-25

[14] Jones, G. C. (1986). *1000 illustrations for preaching and teaching* (p. 293). Nashville, TN: Broadman & Holman Publishers.

[15] Taylor, R. A., & Clendenen, E. R. (2004). *Haggai, Malachi* (Vol. 21A, p. 314). Nashville: Broadman & Holman Publishers.

[16] See Genesis 31:48-53

[17] Goldberg, L. (1999). 198 בָּגַד. (R. L. Harris, G. L. Archer Jr., & B. K. Waltke, Eds.)*Theological Wordbook of the Old Testament.* Chicago: Moody Press.

[18] Taylor, R. A., & Clendenen, E. R. (2004). *Haggai, Malachi* (Vol. 21A, pp. 326–327). Nashville: Broadman & Holman Publishers.

[19] http://www.goodreads.com/quotes/255749-though-the-mills-of-god-grind-slowly-yet-they-grind

[20] *It Pays to Serve Jesus* by Frank Hutson (1909).

[21] *When We See Christ* by Esther L. Kerr Rusthoi (1941).

[22] Morgan, R. J. (2000). *Nelson's complete book of stories, illustrations, and quotes* (electronic ed., pp. 42–43). Nashville: Thomas Nelson Publishers.

[23] Arbesman, Samuel (2012-09-27). The Half-Life of Facts: Why Everything We Know Has an Expiration Date (p. 32). Penguin Group US. Kindle Edition.

[24] Taylor, R. A., & Clendenen, E. R. (2004). *Haggai, Malachi* (Vol. 21A, p. 456). Nashville: Broadman & Holman Publishers.

[25] Terry, Lindsay. (2010). *Stories Behind Popular Hymns.* Grand Rapids: Baker Book Publishers.

[26] http://dailyinfographic.com/divorce-in-america-infographic/divorce-in-america

[27] Morgan, R. J. (2000). *Nelson's complete book of stories, illustrations, and quotes* (electronic ed., p. 801). Nashville: Thomas Nelson Publishers.

[28] Verhoef, Pieter R. (1987). *The Books of Haggai and Malachi.* The New International Commentary on the Old Testament, ed. R.K. Harrison and Robert L. Hubbard, Jr. Grand Rapids, Michigan: William B. Eerdmans.

[29] Hamilton, V. P. (1999). 168 אָרַר. (R. L. Harris, G. L. Archer Jr., & B. K. Waltke, Eds.)*Theological Wordbook of the Old Testament.* Chicago: Moody Press.

[30] Merrill, E. H. (2003). An Exegetical Commentary - Haggai, Zechariah, Malachi (p. 380). Biblical Studies Press.

[31] In Judges 17:5 the Bible describes a house of gods referring to pagan gods. This is not included in the list of 85.

[32] Tan, P. L. (1996). *Encyclopedia of 7700 Illustrations: Signs of the Times* (pp. 478–479). Garland, TX: Bible Communications, Inc.

[33] *Turn Your Eyes Upon Jesus* by Helen Lemmel (1918)

[34] Clark, D. J., & Hatton, H. A. (2002). *A Handbook on Malachi* (p. 433). New York: United Bible Societies.

[35] Verhoef, Pieter R. (1987). *The Books of Haggai and Malachi.* The New International Commentary on the Old Testament, ed. R.K. Harrison and Robert L. Hubbard, Jr. Grand Rapids, Michigan: William B. Eerdmans.

[36] Taylor, R. A., & Clendenen, E. R. (2004). *Haggai, Malachi* (Vol. 21A, pp. 392–393). Nashville: Broadman & Holman Publishers.

[37] Exodus 22:21; 23:12; Leviticus 19:10; 23:22; Deuteronomy 14:29; 24:17; 27:19; Jeremiah 7:6; 22:3; Ezekiel 22:7

[38] http://www.usatoday.com/story/news/world/2014/10/19/pope-francis-synod/17551189/

[39] *Will Jesus Find Us Watching* by Fanny J. Crosby (1876).

[40] Taylor, R. A., & Clendenen, E. R. (2004). *Haggai, Malachi* (Vol. 21A, p. 443). Nashville: Broadman & Holman Publishers.

[41] Merrill, E. H. (2003). An Exegetical Commentary - Haggai, Zechariah, Malachi (p. 387). Biblical Studies Press.

[42] Smith, Alfred B. (1981). *Al Smith's Treasury of Hymn Histories.* Greenville, SC: Better Music Publications, Inc.

[43] Boice, J. M. (2002). The Minor Prophets: an Expositional Commentary (p. 607). Grand Rapids, MI: Baker Books.

[44] Tan, P. L. (1996). *Encyclopedia of 7700 Illustrations: Signs of the Times* (pp. 239–240). Garland, TX: Bible Communications, Inc.

[45] It is Well by Horatio Spafford (1873).

[46] Harrop, C. (2003). Intertestamental History and Literature. In C. Brand, C. Draper, A. England, S. Bond, E. R. Clendenen, & T. C. Butler (Eds.), *Holman Illustrated Bible Dictionary* (p. 830). Nashville, TN: Holman Bible Publishers.

[47] Green, Joel B. (1997) *The Gospel of Luke.* NICNT. Grand Rapids: Eerdmans.

Made in the USA
San Bernardino, CA
30 October 2018